Kayaking with Eric Jackson

Playboating

0 11557 02894 2

Playboating

Eric Jackson

Photos by Skip Brown

Sanctioned by the
World Kayak Federation

STACKPOLE
BOOKS

Published by
STACKPOLE BOOKS
5067 Ritter Road
Mechanicsburg, PA 17055
www.stackpolebooks.com

Printed in China

First Edition

10 9 8 7 6 5 4 3 2

Cover design by Wendy A. Reynolds
All photos by Skip Brown unless otherwise credited

Library of Congress Cataloging-in-Publication Data
Jackson, Eric, 1964–
      Playboating/Eric Jackson.—1st ed.
         p.   cm.—(Kayaking with Eric Jackson)
      ISBN 0-8117-2894-3 (pb)
      1. Kayaking. 2. Kayaking—Competitions. I Title. II Series:
Jackson, Eric, 1964–   Kayaking with Eric Jackson.
GV783.J26 2000
797.1'224—dc21   99-32587
                                                     CIP

*To my true love, my biggest fan, the woman who
makes my life a dream come true, Kristine Jackson.
Thank you for allowing me to be me and for giving me
the two most incredible children on earth, Emily and Dane.*

Contents

CONTENTS

Acknowledgments

This book has a large piece of me in it. It is the culmination of years of commitment to the sport of whitewater rodeo kayaking. The only way to be truly committed to something is to have a bigger reason for being there than the obvious. My reason is the people. Those who keep the rivers of my soul flowing at flood levels are Dane Jackson, Emily Jackson, Mario Vargas, Marc Lyle, Shane Benedict, Clay Wright, Ardnt Schaeflein, Corran Addison, Danny Stock, Scott Shipley, Jamie Simon, Dan Gavere, Opie and Yuk-Yuk, and Ken Whiting.

Thank you to Jesse Stone for helping edit the manuscript. While working on the book in Costa Rica, I handed her ten hours worth of writing each day for two weeks, and she kept up with me every step of the way.

Thanks also to Skip Brown, who drove twelve hours up to the Ottowa at my request and spent a week shooting. As usual, he provided world-class photos.

EJ playboating in the Olympics, slalom style.

Introduction

Employ your time in improving yourself by other men's writings so that you shall come easily by what others have labored hard for.

—Socrates

Years of experience and thought are behind the pages in this book. Most of the ideas come from sources other than myself. Many are EJ originals. All of them are compiled and structured to help you improve your abilities as a playboater or competitive rodeo paddler. If you are hoping to become a better all-around boater, you will find the section on logistics helpful. I also included a section on physical training for paddling, in or out of your boat.

This book gives you the opportunity to learn not only the "how tos" of rodeo moves but also how to excel in any sport; it provides a deeper insight into the process of becoming a champion. You wouldn't be reading this book if you didn't want to improve your abilities. Improving your abilities requires both a logistical plan for acquiring the skills and the on-water tactics to do the moves. This book teaches you how to make a logistical plan for becoming the playboater you want to be. Then the moves are described in detail and broken down into positions and movements for your paddle, boat, and body. Color photos make the moves easy to understand.

When you take what you have learned out to the river, remember that kayaking is just a game—perhaps the greatest game known to humankind. It has all the elements you could want in a game: beautiful settings provided by Mother Nature, who is both on your team and challenging you; tests of skill, speed, adaptability, durability, and patience; and an individual sport that can be played with your friends. Training and playing are the same thing in this sport. Approach this book with the idea that you can learn how to have even more fun on the river than you do now. This way, you are guaranteed to be successful in the game of kayaking. Remember, when you are on the water, you must be happy. Some people take their rodeo paddling too seriously and get anxious and stressed out when they aren't performing at a level acceptable to them. If you get upset when you aren't paddling as well as you'd like, think of this quote from Baltasar Gracián: "It has been said that anxiety does not empty tomorrow of its sorrows, but only empties today of its strength."

PART I

LOGISTICS: ACHIEVING YOUR GOALS IN PLAYBOATING AND RODEO COMPETITION

The difference between the amateur and professional [kayaker]: the amateur focuses on the tactics, and the professional focuses on logistics.
—Paraphrased from Winston Churchill

Rodeo competition is a fun, rewarding way to show off how much you have been playing. Those people who play the hardest tend to do the best in rodeos. You could almost go so far as to say that you can measure somebody's chances of success in rodeo by the amount of fun they've had in their rodeo boat over the past few years. There are many different kinds of rodeos, from the local get-together, where you score one another on a scale of 1 to 10, to the World Championships, where all the best rodeo boaters in the world test their mettle. Rodeo competition is growing like wildfire. There is no telling when it will peak, but it is certainly a long way off.

This section of the book will help you learn the logistics of going from where you are in your skills and ability to where you want to go. To be well rounded in your skills and not become a "one-trick pony," you need to learn all the moves and how to put them together. You need to have a purpose to your playing. Your ultimate goal is to be able to do every move there is, and then start making up some new ones. Exactly how successful you will be in the sport depends on your desire to learn, your true love of the sport, and how often and intensely you play to win. Luckily, a hard day of rodeo training is about as much fun as you can have in a day.

CHAPTER ONE

Becoming Proficient
at Individual Moves

Trifles make perfection, but perfection itself is no trifle.
—Michelangelo

All the moves listed in this book are moves you need to learn. If you are without any of them, you are at a disadvantage in a rodeo. All the hole and wave moves are critical to rodeo competition. It isn't good enough that you can do a move sometimes; you need to be confident that you can do a move every time, on demand. This takes time and attention to each move.

Learning to be a good playboater requires that you go through different phases of development. Becoming proficient at individual moves is a process of layering skills on top of one another. Each move has certain prerequisite basic skills. For example, to front surf a wave, you have to be able to do a ferry before you can even get onto a wave. To cartwheel, you need to position yourself on top of the foampile of a hole, do initiation strokes on demand, lead with your head and body, and possess edge control. You must have the basic skills in your subconscious so that you have enough brainpower left to focus consciously on the new moves you are trying to learn. Like a computer, you have only a certain amount of random-access memory (RAM). This means that you can focus on only a limited number of things at once—usually, two. Therefore, if you are trying to learn to do a splitwheel, it

will be impossible unless you can enter the hole, get yourself set up, and initiate the bow without much conscience thought. A good way to know that you are out of RAM is when everything is happening too fast. You are in a hole and the water is splashing everywhere, your boat is bouncing around, and you want to pull over to the corner of the hole to do a spin, but you pull yourself right out of the hole. This is a sign that you don't have enough hole-surfing experience committed to your subconscious to do that move. You'll know that you are increasing your brainpower for playboating when the waves or holes you are surfing start to slow down and become manageable. This process can be quick or it may take a while, depending on whether you focus on the basics. Playing the same wave or hole over and over again is the best way to see the process in action. Over the long term, you will constantly be adding to your experience; the easier moves will become automatic and won't take up any RAM. This frees your brain up to focus on new moves and techniques. For example: you need to do a spin to set up a cartwheel in a particular hole. You won't be successful with the cartwheel if you need all your RAM (brainpower) to focus on the spin. But if the spin is automatic, you can focus on timing your initiation and the technique for the cartwheel. It keeps layering after that. If you want to do a five-point cartwheel into a split, you can forget it if you have to focus on the spin first.

The moves are ordered from easiest to hardest in each chapter. Your goal is to commit each move to your subconscious, starting with the easier ones. The new skills you learn will layer on top of the previous ones. You will soon be able to focus clearly and be in control of everything that is going on while you are surfing and setting up moves in a hole. After more practice and committing more basic skills and moves to your subconscious, you will be able to control the larger, bouncier, crazier waves and holes as if you were sitting on your sofa and surfing the television with your remote. It is all a function of what skills you have committed to your subconscious through repetition and training in the basics.

In 1999, there were thousands of kayakers who had the skills in a hole or on a wave that perhaps only twenty people had in 1993. Of course, by 1999, those twenty people had increased their subconscious powers way beyond their 1993 levels. To catch up to the best boaters requires a systematic approach to learning all the basics, then layering on those skills until all the skills have been acquired. It can be done. Look at Rusty Sage, who at only eighteen years old won the Pre–World Championships in New Zealand in 1998 against the best boaters in the world. How did he catch up? It is easy to catch up to someone who is blazing a path in a jungle, because the path is already there to run on. The leaders aren't running on any path; they are inching along, cutting away with their machetes. Once you catch up to the leaders, it is tough to get ahead, because you are faced with the same situation they

are. All progress becomes unknown territory and comes with more difficulty. But once you get to that point, you have more time to hone those basics.

FOCUS ON BASICS

Good habits are as addictive as bad habits, and a lot more rewarding. —Anonymous

Good basic paddling character is critical to almost every move you do. Proper strokes and basic body positions make learning the moves much easier. Trying to learn difficult moves without a solid foundation won't work. Each move has basics that must be done properly if the move is to be done consistently.

The following kayaking rules will ensure that you have the basics to enjoy rapid growth in your playboating skills. These rules are not intended to inhibit your own style or personality but to prevent you from trying to break the laws of physics and getting frustrated. (I suggest that you read my previous book, *Whitewater Paddling: Strokes and Concepts,* before continuing on with this one.)

Lead every turn with your head and body. Your head and body position is the single most important factor in learning the moves in playboating. Here is why:

- By leading with you head and body, you more than double the time that you can see the target you are aiming for.
- Your boat wants to follow your head and body; therefore, it will go where you have pointed them.
- You have much more physical leverage on your strokes when your body is wound like a spring.
- Your strokes are in proper position when your head and body are leading.

- If you are leading with your head and body, you are ahead of the move; if not, you are behind, and it is very difficult to catch up.

Keep your weight over the boat. Your body weight should be supported by your butt on your seat. Bracing is a wonderful thing to keep you from falling over, but you can't do rodeo moves when bracing. The need to brace comes primarily from intentionally throwing your weight around. Any body movement that gets you off balance should be avoided. Almost all braces can be avoided by keeping your weight centered over the boat. For example: When side surfing a hole, can you keep your paddle out of the water, or do you have to brace on it? You need to be able to sit flat on the water with no brace (weight over the boat, boat flat to the water). Spinning, cartwheeling, and the like should all be done without the need to brace for balance. Before the playboating revolution started, big, deep braces and never flipping were signs of a good boater. The good boaters of the past have to learn how to keep their bodies still.

Get a good rodeo boat. Nothing will hinder your ability to learn the playboating moves more than equipment that can't perform the moves. People say to me all the time, "I'll get a new rodeo boat once I start learning how to do more moves. At this point in my paddling career, I don't need the latest boat." There is nothing further from the truth. Rodeo boats progress so quickly because we are trying to make the moves we are doing easier and the moves we want to do possible. The next generation of boats will make the new moves easier and newer ones possible. If you buy an outdated boat, you are making current moves impossible (even for the best of us) and older moves more difficult. Every rodeo boat from five years ago is now a beginner boat or a general all-around boat. Remember that you can run rivers in a boat you are comfortable with. And after a number of times in a new boat, you will be comfortable with it, and your old boat will be obsolete.

Big Kahuna on the Ottawa River. Good basics equals more fun.

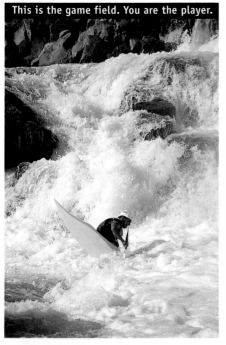

This is the game field. You are the player.

A short, sweet commute to the play spots of the Potomac River.

KEEP STATISTICS ON YOUR CURRENT ABILITIES AND PROGRESS

The surest road to inspiration is preparation. —Lloyd George

Experience is not what happens to a man; it is what a man does with what happens to him.
—Aldous Huxley

When practicing moves, have a system for measuring your ability and progress. Each move can be measured for consistency. Some, such as cartwheels, can be measured in quantity. Your memory of a day of training or playing is usually selective. You often remember your best ride and what frustrated you most. If you hope to be better than you are now, keeping statistics on your training is the most rewarding, and productive method of measuring your progress. You will not be able to detect the smaller improvements otherwise. I suggest the following system for monitoring your improvement. When you use this system with your friends, it can easily be done as a game.

If you have decided to work on right-hand cartwheels, give yourself five tries to initiate the bow and see how many ends you can link off each initiation. You then get an average number of ends per initiation. For example: You go into the hole and initiate the bow but do only a two-pointer. Your next try you get a six-pointer. Your next three tries you get a four, a one, and a two. You did a total of fifteen ends in five tries for an average of three ends per initiation. This means that at this time, you are a three-end person to the right in that hole. You may have gotten a six-pointer, but that is not your average. Obviously, your goal is to improve your average. You should do this exercise with every move you know. Get your averages off the stern, for splits,

EJ still finds interesting things to do when he's not playboating.
PHOTO BY COLIN MEAGHER

your averages. You can quantify your mastery of every move you practice by getting your averages. If you have improved, you'll be rewarded by seeing your better numbers. If you haven't improved, you'll know that you haven't learned anything about that move since the last time, or maybe you just had an off day.

When practicing individual moves, always remind yourself what basics you are working on. Don't get into the habit of just trying a move and seeing what you do wrong. Try to focus on what you want to do right. If you get that right, add something else you want to get right about the move. Eventually, you will be able to do almost everything right for that move.

DO REMEDIAL TRAINING

> *The best fortune that can come*
> *to a man is that which corrects*
> *his defects and makes up for*
> *his failings.* —Goethe

for loops, and so forth. If a move is a single-shot move (such as a loop), do five tries and get an average for success. For example, if you try to do a loop five times and get two loops, that is a 40 percent average. There are numerous reasons to use this technique and document your averages: It is a reality check on your skill at a particular move, it allows you to monitor your improvement, and it helps you make routines. (You wouldn't, for example, decide to put a ten-point cartwheel in your routine if your average is only four.) The most important thing to know in rodeo is how to link cartwheels and split them on demand. You should get your averages to the left, to the right, off the bow, off the stern, and off a split for every rodeo site you go to. Also, anyplace you get to practice often is a good place to get

Practice the moves that are giving you the most trouble. Most rodeo boaters are always trying to take what they are best at and make it better. Although this can be fun, it leaves the rest of your skills in the dirt. You need to be good at all the moves. If you are not, it will be apparent at the next rodeo. Also, by always working on your weakest moves first, you will be sure to practice a larger number of moves in a day. The less skill you have in a move, the faster you can improve that move, since there is more to learn. Your growth curve will be steeper for moves you haven't spent a lot of time working on. This means that you will notice more improvements when doing remedial training. Coming off the river feeling like you've learned something is always rewarding.

GET ON DIFFERENT WATER

Variety's the very spice of life.
—William Cowper

If you paddle on only one river when you are learning rodeo moves, you will find that you don't do nearly as well on new rivers. Getting on lots of different rivers not only is more fun but also improves your ability to do well at any playspot. Most people I know do best on their home rivers. Most boaters who don't get to travel don't paddle at the same level at a new river as they do at home. They usually look like different boaters in a new river.

Cutting water.

CHAPTER TWO

Learning to Link Different Moves

Certain moves go well with others. Either they make the next move easy to do, or they take little time to set up after the last move. The ultimate rides are one long flurry of linked moves with no break in the action. You can't do this without some understanding of what goes together.

KNOW WHICH MOVES GO WELL TOGETHER

Some moves naturally set you up for another move. These compatible moves are good to practice together because in a rodeo, it is important to keep the flow going. Other moves require some setting up, and these are best done after a compatible move. Moves that don't go well together can be done back to back, but it takes a lot more time and effort.

The following moves go well together:
- Spin right into cartwheel right (and vice versa)
- Cartwheel left into split right (and vice versa)
- Split right into cartwheel right (and vice versa)
- Blunt left into cartwheel left off stern (and vice versa)

- Retendo into spin or blast (a retendo is usually a missed cartwheel, so the spin keeps the boat moving as you land sideways into the hole)
- Cartwheels into loop (and vise versa)

Some moves don't go well together because they take too much time, aren't worth many points, or force you to take a break in the action. For example:
- Front blunt left into front blunt right (same for back blunts)
- Spin right into spin left (you usually have to surf to the other side of the hole)
- Cartwheel right into spin left (and vice versa)
- Split from left to right into anything to the left (and vice versa)
- Anything into a side surf

USE MOVES AS YOUR SAFETY NET

It is always good to know which moves you can hit a high percentage of the time and feel confident in. These moves can be your safety net. When your routine doesn't go as planned, you can always do your default move and continue to get points while you set up for the rest of your routine. For example: If cartwheels to the left are a move that I can do well in a particular hole, I may use them as my safety net move. When I am doing my routine in a rodeo and I get out of control, I immediately do left cartwheels to get set up for the move I just missed. This way, I am still getting points while I collect myself. Make sure that you pick a move that you can do on demand and will earn you some points while you regroup. Don't make a side surf your default position, because the side surf is worth zero points. The front blast is a good safety move, because you can almost always get into a front blast from any position, even immediately after rolling up. Additionally, you can do almost any move quickly from a front blast.

Every move is a stepping stone to the next move.

CHAPTER THREE

Creating Routines for Competition

Great battles are won before they are actually fought.
—John Lubbock

It is almost impossible to win a major competition without a good routine. Routines eliminate the need to remember what moves you have done and what moves you need to do. It is extremely important to understand the current rodeo rules and create a routine that will maximize your score based on those rules. The specific values of different moves and other factors of the scoring system are always evolving.

USE YOUR STRENGTHS

Mediocrity obtains more with application than superiority without it. —Baltasar Gracián

Competition is no time for remedial training. Now is the time to put your best foot forward and hope that the moves you are good at are enough to make a good routine. How do you decide whether you are good enough at a move to include it in your routine? Check your averages. Before the competition, you should try every move you think is possible at the rodeo site to see what you can do successfully and what you have problems with. If you have enough time before the competition to fix all your problem moves, you will be able to choose from every available move when you make your routine.

Unfortunately, this is not usually the case, even for the best rodeo boaters in the world. This means that you should rank your moves in order of the ones you are most likely to pull off to least likely. At some sites, there are only a limited number of moves available; these are easy to rank. At the best sites, every move in this book is available, so you need to give yourself a couple of days to prepare the list. For one-shot moves such as loops, clean cartwheels, and blunts, you simply rank them in order of percentage of success (for example, if you are three out of five for left bow blunts, your success rate is 60 percent). Any move at 60 percent or higher is one that you are likely to pull off. If you can cartwheel, then you are probably near 100 percent for a front surf or a spin, so they will be at the top of your list. Cartwheels are a little different. If your average is four points per initiation to the left, you should try five three-pointers to see what your average is. Then you can rank your cartwheels as "three-point cartwheels, left." For splitwheels, get your averages for splitting right-left and left-right off the first bow, the third bow, and so on, if you can. You should not count on hitting a splitwheel if your average is less than 80 percent (for example, if you average 100 percent for right-left splits off the first bow, 80 percent off the third bow, and 60 percent off the fifth bow, you should plan on splitting on your third end for your routine and rank your right-left split-wheel as an 80 percent move).

Now you have a comprehensive list of moves and your percentages for hitting them. With this list you have the tools to make the highest-scoring routine you can expect to accomplish, given your specific skills. The challenge is to make a solid routine from this list. If your time limit is only thirty seconds, you will likely not have enough time to do all the moves on your "above 60 percent" list. Your objective is to get the highest possible technical score while maximizing your multiplier. This means that you need to constantly be performing different moves. Ideally, these moves have high multipliers, and allow you to accrue as many technical points as you can. Here is the list I used to come up with my routine for the 1998 Pre–World Preliminary rides (multipliers are in parentheses): front surf 100 percent (.25),

back surf 100 percent (.25), spin right 100 percent (.25), spin left 100 percent (.25), blunt left bow 100 percent (.75), blunt right bow 100 percent (.75), cartwheel left (6 points) 80 percent (.75), cartwheel right (3 points) 80 percent (.75), clean spin left 80 percent (.5), shuvit left-right 80 percent (.5), back blunt left 60 percent (.75), back blunt right 60 percent (.75), clean cartwheel left (2 points) 60 percent (1), split right-left (off third end) 60 percent (1), split left-right (off fifth end) 60 percent (1), Ollie 40 percent (.75), back loop 20 percent (1), front loop 20 percent (1), aerial blunt 20 percent (1).

CREATE AN ORDER OF MOVES FOR MAXIMUM UPSIDE, MINIMUM DOWNSIDE POTENTIAL

The next step is to choose the highest-scoring moves and decide how you can choreograph them to create the most time-efficient and successful routine. The routine will be your expression of what you can do with what you have. The routine I devised from the list above was this:

MOVE	POINTS	MULTIPLIER
Shuvit left-right for the entry move	2	0.50
Blunt left off bow	4	0.75
Cartwheel left off stern (linked to blunt; 6 ends)	24	0.75
Split right off left cartwheels	8	1.00
Cartwheel right off split (2 more ends)	8	0.75
Blunt left off bow	4	0.75
Stern ender linked to blunt	4	0.50
Elevated shuvit right-left linked to ender	4	0.50
Cartwheel left (3 ends)	12	0.00
Split right	8	0.00
TOTAL	**78 points x 6.5 = 507 points**	

At the point of the elevated shuvit, I was twenty to twenty-eight seconds into the ride, and my multiplier was about as high as I could get it unless I hit a loop or other low-percentage move. The spins and surfs wouldn't have added as much to my score as increasing my technical score with some cartwheels and splits, so I finished with them.

With two judges, this routine adds up to 1,014 points. The routine could also be awarded a bonus of up to 10 percent for style. Thus the overall potential for the routine is 1,115 points.

My best score was 722 doing this routine. Why was it lower? I did every move listed, but some of my cartwheels weren't vertical, and I didn't always get both splits for my multiplier because one end wasn't vertical enough. At the end, I ran out of time before I got all the extra points for the cartwheels and split. But it is better to make your routine longer than the time limit so you don't give up any points by finishing early.

Coming up with a routine that works for your skill level can be done in numerous ways. The way I believe works the best is this:

1. Pick an entry move that will earn you points in the first second of your ride and for which your success rate is at least 80 percent. You can't afford to blow the entry move. Choose one with as high a multiplier as possible. (For example, I chose the shuvit because it has a multiplier of .5. My only other options were a spin or a surf at a multiplier of .25 and the same technical score.)

2. Do your highest-scoring 80 percent or better moves next. If you are going to blow out on a move, you might as well get some points doing it.

3. Finish with the moves that are left but aren't as high scoring, such as spins, surfs, and blunts.

4. If you have the luxury of a five-second buzzer, throw in a high-risk move (40 to 60 percent) that you haven't done yet. (A 20 percent move is not likely to pay off, so avoid it.) It is better to double up on moves you can do and increase your technical score. I usually like to throw loops, but I wasn't good enough at them at the New Zealand site to include them in my routine (only 20 percent success rate).

After you set your routine, you need to find out how long it takes and whether you can pull it off. You then need to make adjustments to the routine before the competition. The process you go through from planning a routine on paper to executing a fully developed routine you feel confident in is as follows:

1. Do the first half of your routine five times, and time each run. Determine a percentage of success (it is often zero). Don't panic if the percentage is low. How long did it take?

2. Now (unless you included a move that you have decided you can't do successfully), practice the first half of the routine for percentage of success, concurrently reducing the time it takes. Give yourself ten or more practice runs to learn the routine and be able to perform the moves without difficulty.

3. Do the same for the second half of the routine. Do not combine the two parts yet. If the average time it takes you to complete each section adds up to less than the alotted time, you need to add a move or two. You should add a high-percentage and a high-technical-scoring move. If your ride is taking too long, determine what moves

aren't going to make it before you run out of time. If these moves are critical to your score (high multiplier, high technical score, and high percentage), swap them with a less important move earlier in your routine.

LEARN TO DO YOUR ROUTINE SUCCESSFULLY

Patience and fortitude conquer all things.
—Ralph Waldo Emerson

Now, it is time to practice your revised routine as a whole. Do sets of five, getting your percentage on each one. Don't be too hard on yourself. If you hit most of the moves and don't flush out, you are doing well. If you aren't getting anywhere near the end of the routine without flushing, you need to either make the routine easier or focus better. It may take a while to get it right. With most rodeos, you are lucky to get a few hours in the hole before it starts. You will just have to abbreviate the process.

Once you have the routine up to 60 percent or better, you are ready to compete. Remember that finals typically count only the best of two runs. So theoretically, a success rate of 60 percent almost guarantees that you will have one good ride. Of course, real life doesn't always work that way. The preliminaries usually count both rides. Do your best to nail both of them. If you hit your routine on only one ride, you still will likely make the finals if your routine is high-scoring enough.

If you are having difficulty with a move in your routine that you normally do well, do it separately until you get it dialed in again. Usually, if you work on it a few times focusing on the basics, you will be up to speed in no time. Then go back to your routine.

Having trouble getting past one move in your routine? Brush up on it, then start over.

There's nothing like competing to make you feel alive! Photo by Colin Meagher

CHAPTER FOUR

Training for Competition

*It is fine to aim high if we have developed the ability to
accomplish our aims, but there is no use aiming unless
our gun is loaded.*

—William Ross

The secrete of success is constancy to purpose.
—Benjamin Disraeli

Nothing in this book will have an effect on your boating unless you put the ideas to work. In rodeo kayaking, training and playing are interchangeable, as long as there is purpose behind your playing. Most of your training for competition can be done on almost any river you venture to. Some rivers offer more playspots and higher-quality playspots. The more training you do on better rivers, the more you can learn. The most important factor in your ability to compete is a long-term plan. Learning how to do all the rodeo moves and how to package that knowledge into your competition rides must be included in your plan. Below is a list of things you need to do to become a good competitor.

PRACTICE COMPETING

The best way to ensure that you know how to compete well is to practice competing. You can do this with almost any rodeo boater who enjoys competing. You can keep the competitions simple, such as who can link the most ends to the right, or make them more complex, such as a mock rodeo. You may find that your performance level goes down immediately when you start competing. This is a sure sign that you need to become more comfortable competing. (If you don't enjoy competing, you need to eliminate competition from your life and just learn playboating for your personal pleasure.) Practice in forming routines is an important part of your training to compete. You can make a routine at your local playspot and practice it once or twice when you go out. It takes hours to gather the data for a routine, so it won't be something you forget easily.

KEEP COMPETITION FUN

*A man can succeed at almost
anything for which he has
unlimited enthusiasm.*
—Charles Schwab

No matter how high you are aiming in your competitive career, each step of the way must be enjoyable. You can't suffer through years of training with the idea that it will be fun once you make it to the top. First, there is no top. No matter how high you get, you will try to get higher. This means that you will never be happy if you aren't happy now. There are lots of dismal activities you can partake in that have more substantial material rewards than kayak competition. Kayaking is too special not to be enjoyed to the fullest every day. So if you want to be a competitor, you had better enjoy as many aspects of the competition as you can.

Some of the more rewarding aspects of kayaking are:

- Meeting lots of great people
- Participating in one of the most supportive competitive enviornments in any sport
- Competing in a sport that is directly related to one of your favorite recreational activities—playboating
- Traveling to interesting places

I'm sure you can come up with your own list of reasons why competition is fun and why training for competition is equally fun.

STAY FOCUSED

*Fidelity to a worthy purpose is
what constitutes true happiness*
—Helen Keller

*Readiness for opportunity makes
for success. Opportunity often
comes by accident, readiness
never does.* —Samuel Rayburn

If you keep your kayaking skills in the forefront of your mind at all times when you are playboating, not only during training sessions, you will be more likely to take advantage of the many opportunities to improve. Being focused means knowing your weaknesses and looking for opportunities to improve those areas. It is being aware of when the local rodeo hero is going out to play and tagging along to learn something. You will not be happy if you let opportunities slip by because you weren't focused on your long-term goal. Grab opportunities when they come, and create opportunities when possible. Each time you go out to play on the river, know what you want to achieve during your run. (Maybe it is just a fun creek run with little play but lots of great rock spins.) If you are unable to train in the winter, make your training plan for the spring, lift weights, run, watch kayaking videos, and stay in the loop. Don't get stale, stay focused.

Remember, those watching and judging are your friends. PHOTO BY COLIN MEAGHER

CHAPTER FIVE

Competition Day

Definiteness of purpose is the starting point of all achievement.
—Clement Stone

Doing your best should be your purpose in any competition. You can't affect how others do, so you must concentrate on your own performance. Measure your success against how well you think you could score on your routine. If you did your preparatory work, you will know how many points you could potentially get during your ride. You will also know how well you did your routine compared with training runs. This is how you measure your results at the end of the day. Ultimately, you may decide that your goal is to score higher than anyone else in the competition. You will know whether that is possible by knowing your capability and that of your competition. You may also factor in whether you have a better logistical plan than your competition. Most of your competitors don't have a plan that allows them to maximize their skills on competition day. You can beat people who are better than you if you have a better plan.

ELIMINATE UNKNOWNS

You need to know as much about the competition beforehand as possible. Is there water for practice? Parking near the hole? Food? Drinks? What rules are being used? What is the schedule for the competition? When do you have to pick up your bib? Can you judge if you want to? Talk to the variety judges and make sure that they are judging the way you think they are. Plan your day so that there are no avoidable surprises. Plan for a full day at the river; assume that the competition will be delayed for hours and that you will have to wait.

MAKE A SOLID LOGISTICAL PLAN

Your plan should include the following:
1. When you will practice and warm up for your rides
2. When you will register and set up to compete
3. When and where you will eat
4. When and where you will watch the competition
5. When and where you will rest
6. When you will talking to the judges about how moves are being called (primarily the variety judges)
7. When you will have to compete (make an educated guess, double-check periodically to see if the heats are going according to your prediction, and make adjustments as needed)
8. When you will talk with fellow competitors to make sure that they don't know something important that you don't

Relaxed focus is generally the best state of mind for competition day.
PHOTO BY COLIN MEAGHER

Take all this information and make your basic plan for the day and for your rides. You will be less stressed than those who don't know what is going on. You will also be in control of your day. Your research may turn up some important piece of information. Remember, you will never perform better than you hoped. If you do, you were not expecting much from yourself.

BE RESTED

Get enough sleep the night before. Don't watch every ride in the competition; watching is stressful. Take a nap before your ride if possible.

STAY FOCUSED

> It has been said that our worry doesn't empty tommorrow of its sorrow, but only rids today of its strength.
> —Charles Haddon Spurgeon

Many influences will try to pull you away from your plan, but stick to it as closely as possible. Try to avoid emotional conflicts; they drain your mental resources. Take your mind off the competition, unless you need to think about it as part of being focused. Listen to music, talk with friends, or take a nap when you have done everything you need to do to prepare. Don't worry about how you will do. Be happy that you get to show off your skills.

CHAPTER SIX

Competing to Your Potential

You can not teach a man anything; you can only help him to find it for himself.

—Galileo

Everyone is different when it comes to competition day. What helps one person relax will stress another out. However, there are several factors that seem to be consistent among all people for achieving optimal performance under the pressure of competition.

LEARN TO ACHIEVE YOUR OPTIMAL STATE OF MIND

Everyone has a level of excitement that is optimal for them. For some, it is totally laid back; for others, getting pumped up helps them focus. (You can't achieve your optimal state of mind unless you know what that is.) List all your best rides in practice and competition, and then determine what your state of mind was immediately before the rides. Were you joking around, or were you serious? Were you nervous or relaxed? Once you have determined the answers to those questions, plan on being in that state of mind for your competition rides.

STICK TO YOUR PLAN

Insist on yourself, never imitate.
—Ralph Waldo Emerson

You made a good plan before the competition, so have confidence in it. Everyone else in the competition will have a different plan. People better than you will offer suggestions on what you should do differently, but the day of the competition is not the time to change your plan. You are more likely to do well with a practiced plan that isn't perfect than with an improvised "perfect" plan. Also, you will have more confidence and hence be more relaxed during your rides.

COMPETE AT YOUR "VOLLEY PACE"

Top tennis players control the volley pace to keep it at their speed. Everyone has a pace that he can keep under control in a hole. The tendency for rodeo boaters is to try to compete at a faster pace than they are used to practicing. This results in premature flushing and missed moves. Sometimes, you may be tempted to take extra time to set up because the competition is "important" and you don't want to make a mistake. This is slower than your normal "volley pace," and you will be just as likely to mess up going too slow as too fast.

FOCUS ON THE TASK AT HAND

You have no control over anything but your ride as you enter the hole. The judging, other competitors' rides, and what place you will get are all beyond your control. It is counterproductive to worry

Why are you here? Putting fun first and performance second is the surest way to perform well.

about the results when you haven't even done your rides yet. Obviously, you would be happier with a good result than a bad one, but the time to think about results is after you have completed your rides. If you've had a terrible first ride, then all you can do is to be ready for your next ride. (Your last ride is done and the scores are already recorded, so there is nothing you can do about it.) Your next ride is all you have control over. You know from practice that some rides will be better than others. Don't let a bad ride change your attitude. If you are focused on the fact that you blew the first ride, what are the chances that your second ride is going to be good? Not very high. Keep your ideal state of mind.

ENJOY YOURSELF

Learning to be relaxed enough to enjoy competition day is critical to your long-term enjoyment of the sport. It is easy to get all worked up on competition day and not enjoy the feeling. Many people only feel relieved when the competition is over. You should be looking forward to the next competition because the day has been fun and rewarding. All the feelings you experience during the competition are part of being totally alive—not comfortably numb. Enjoy a good laugh with fellow competitors in your heat. They are feeling the same things you are and hope to do well, just like you. Helping your competitors relax will relax you as well. Enjoy the emotional roller coaster, because it is one of the best parts of competition.

PART II

TACTICS:
THE RODEO MOVES

The list of moves is always growing. Thanks to the natural athletes in this sport equipped with imagination and the finest skills, the sport continues to grow at a phenomenal pace. A common misconception is that the best rodeo boaters are trying to do something new just for the sake of naming a move or being different. This is not the case. We are out on the river having as much fun as possible. In so doing, we like to see what we can get away with on whatever features are available, sometimes crashing and flushing out of a playspot. Just when you think that there is nothing new that can be done on a river, a boater proves you wrong. The same is true for boat design. If you keep an open mind, you will not become stale or bored and may come up with new ideas yourself. This part of the book is the how-to section on the rodeo moves. It discusses all the current rodeo moves, generally moving from easy moves to harder ones. The easier moves are written with less experienced playboaters in mind. The sections on the more advanced moves are written for the boaters who will be practicing those moves.

CHAPTER SEVEN

Wave Moves

Surfing's the sauce, it will change your life.

—Point Break

T he front surf and back surf are the basic play moves that have made kayaking so incredibly fun.

MOVE	Front Surf
WKF DEFINITION	**Showing that you are established on the wave by doing a cutback or surfing for three or more seconds.**
WKF SCORING	**1 technical point;**
	.25 is added to your variety multiplier.

GETTING ON A WAVE

Each wave is different, varying in speed, steepness, shallowness, and accessibility. Wave surfing revolves around putting your boat on the wave and adjusting for those factors. Getting on a wave is simply a ferry from an eddy to the wave. The goal is to ferry into the sweet spot on the wave. The sweet spot is where your boat can be in equilibrium, where gravity and the oncoming water forces are balanced. This spot is not in the trough of the wave but somewhere on the face of it. A good ferry in which you are in control of your angle and boat position from the time you begin to cross the eddyline until you are established on the wave is essential to successful surfing.

Steps for Getting on a Wave:

1. Start low enough in the eddy and below the wave to get some speed to cross the eddyline.
2. Spot (turn your head and look at) your target—the sweet spot on the wave.
3. Ferry to that sweet spot using peel-out and ferry technique. Use the proper peel-out technique of pulling yourself across the eddyline with a forward stroke into an open-faced stern draw until you get to the sweet spot.
4. You are now established on the wave.

What does the sweet spot look like? For most waves, the sweet spot is usually where the wave is the largest and steepest. However, for particularly steep waves, the sweet spot can be found where it isn't so steep. Your goal is to learn to read the water so that you know what the sweet spot looks like. As your skills increase, you will be able to surf more of the wave, and the sweet spot becomes a safety net for you.

Common Mistakes Made for Getting on a Wave:

1. *Peeling out above the wave and dropping back into it.* This technique puts you at the mercy of the wave, is much more physically demanding, and puts you blindly onto the wave. The only time you enter a wave from above is when it is not possible to enter from the side. If the wave is way out in the middle of the river or you are catching it on the fly (while floating downstream), you have no choice but to enter it from above (see later for entering waves from upstream).

2. *Not keeping your eyes fixed on the target.* Most people who have trouble catching waves have their eyes fixed straight over the bow and see only the oncoming water and the bow. As a result, the bow is lost downstream or pushed back into the eddy. This causes them to peel out too high or too low from the eddy. It is always easier to hit your target if you are looking at it ahead of time.

3. *Improper strokes when exiting the eddy.* Remember to always take a forward stroke on the downstream side to pull your butt all the way across the eddyline. Convert it into a stern draw to control the ferry out to the wave. Many people try to rudder onto the wave from the eddyline. This is a low-percentage technique that will not get you on the wave as often.

Getting on a Wave from Above

The first step is to get in front of the sweet spot (the steepest and largest part of the wave). Keep your boat sideways enough to see the sweet spot as you float toward it and make final adjustments in your approach to ensure that you hit the sweet spot. For catching a wave on the fly, the technique is as follows: Just as you get about four seconds from the wave, turn your boat upstream and take some medium hard strokes. As you feel yourself dropping into the trough of the wave, paddle almost full speed; as you feel yourself rising up the face, sprint all out. You should be able to stop your downstream momentum and catch the wave. Timing is everything, and most people sprint too early. Sprint when you are in the trough and rising up the face. Keep your body weight forward until you are surfing back upstream on the wave.

SURFING AROUND ON A WAVE

For the most part, surfing occurs on waves that don't have a large surfable area. Any direction you move will eventually lead you off the wave. When entering a wave, you need to have your eyes on the sweet spot, because your goal is to put your butt on top of it. If you notice that you are moving downstream of the sweet spot, paddle harder; if you are moving forward of it, paddle slower.

The smaller the wave, the more difficult it is to stay on it without surfing skills. Once you are on the sweet spot of the wave, you must go somewhere else immediately (unless you are paddling a boat that will not pearl or the wave is big enough to let you sit there). You control where you go on a wave. You can go left, right, up, or down, or you can spin around backward. When you turn either left or right, you will automatically be lifted up to the top of the wave. When you surf straight on, you will drop down into the trough of the wave. Planing-hulled boats are more forgiving

1. Forward stroke to begin cut.

2. Inside lean, weight forward, to create speed.

3. Rudder and inside lean to begin aggressive cutback.

4. Rudder and outside lean to finish aggressive cutback.

for surfing because you don't have to worry about overturning. If you turn too much, they slide sideways and stay on the wave instead of peeling off it.

TYPES OF FRONT SURFING
Parking
Parking is dropping into the trough and sitting there. You have probably done this before. It is very satisfying because you don't have to do anything except enjoy the rush of water. To park, you need a boat that will blast a wave—the more rocker, the better. Ferry out to the sweet spot and let yourself drop into the trough. Then lean back and enjoy the equilibrium. Your boat will automatically settle in the trough. Use small rudder strokes on either side to keep the boat straight. Most boats will stay straight anyhow.

Cutting
Surfing back and forth on the wave is called cutting. There are varying degrees of cutting (mild, medium, or aggressive).

Note that most boats will assist you in turning on a wave if you lean the boat in the direction you want to turn. For example, if you lean the boat to the left, it will turn left, unless the boat is off at a sharp angle.

Paddle position and movement
- *Mild cutting:* Rudder left until the boat is pointed left. Rudder right before the boat surfs off the side of the wave and the boat is pointed right. Repeat as many times as desired.
- *Medium cutting:* Rudder harder so the boat will surf off the wave unless you rudder it back the other way almost immediately. A forward stroke may be needed after each rudder to stay on the wave.
- *Aggressive cutting:* Rudder as hard as possible, followed by a forward stroke on the same side to keep you on the wave and bring you back across the face. The technique is the same as medium cutting, but with more

emphasis placed on speed and staying near the peak of the wave. The greatest boat speed can be had near the peak of the wave.

Body position and movement
- *Mild cutting:* Keep your weight back to prevent the bow from going under on smaller waves. On larger ones, keep your weight neutral.
- *Medium cutting:* Keep your body neutral, except when using a rudder. Lean forward when using a rudder (the same position as a reverse sweep; parallel to the boat, back at the stern). Turn your boat to the side by prying the stern away from the paddle. The more aggressive your turning strokes, the higher you will pull yourself up on the wave and the more likely that you will need forward strokes to keep you on the wave. The best combination of rudder and forward strokes for cutting is rudder on the left and then a forward stroke on the left; repeat on the right. The forward stroke increases speed and makes the surf more dynamic.
- *Aggressive cutting:* Your body moves forward to neutral and back to forward with precise timing to make the boat respond more quickly. Stay neutral until your boat turns past the direction of the oncoming water, then throw your weight forward to get the bow down on the water so it will accelerate you the other way. Once you put in a forward stroke, sit upright until you begin to turn back again. The goal is to keep the boat ends out of the water by keeping your body neutral. Once you have made most of your turn, drop the bow for forward speed.

Boat position and movement
- *Mild cutting:* Keep your boat nearly flat and near the trough of the wave. Lean the downstream edge in the water only enough to keep you from catching the upstream edge and pearling.
- *Medium cutting:* Same as for mild cutting, but with more downstream lean, which rides you up the face of the wave and increases the boat speed. The change from leaning on one edge to the other is done just as you cut the other way.
- *Aggressive cutting:* Throw your boat with all your strength for aggressive cutting. The more strength you use, the more aggressive the cut and the more dynamic your surf. Start in a normal surf, then rudder the boat to 45 degrees, letting the boat rise to the top of the wave. Keep the downstream edge in the water until you are ready to cut the other way or you are almost out of the wave. As soon as you begin your rudder, throw your weight back to the neutral position, switch your boat's downstream lean to an upstream lean, and begin to drop the bow down (your bow will be in the air, since you have a sharp angle and have been rising up the wave). Your goal is to get the bow down into the water and the downstream edge in as soon as possible. The faster the transition from surfing one way to cutting back and dropping the bow to surf the other way, the more exciting the surf. Most people don't drop their edges in the water, so the boat doesn't have much acceleration down and across the wave immediately following the cut.

MOVE	Back surf
WKF DEFINITION	A back surf is credited when you have shown that you are "established" on the wave by either doing a cutback or remaining in the back surf position for three or more seconds.
WKF SCORING	2 technical points; .25 is added to your variety multiplier.

Controlling your back surf is one of playboating's biggest challenges. As the wave gets more difficult or "crazy" (as Ken Whiting would say), the task becomes more challenging. Back surfing is more difficult than front surfing because

1. It is more difficult to see.
2. You don't spend as much of your paddling time in the backward position, so you are not as proficient backward.
3. Many boat designs are not symmetrical from front to back and are designed to surf frontward better than backward. A symmetrical boat is best.

There are no physical or technical reasons you can't back surf as well as you front surf. You just need to spend more time practicing back surfing to get your ability up to speed. You can either park or cut while back surfing.

PARKING

The technique is the same as for front surfing, except that you lean forward when on the wave to keep the stern from burying. You can look downstream and to either side to see that your boat stays straight. It is too difficult to turn around to look at your stern when parking.

Paddle position and movement. Place your rudder in the water at the bow with the power face away from the boat. The paddle movements are sweeps from the bow with the paddle as parallel to the side of the boat as possible (same concept as the rudder while front surfing). To keep the boat straight, switch your ruddering from left to right and back again as needed.

Body position and movement. Keep your weight forward and over the boat.

Boat position and movement. Keep your boat flat and pointed straight downstream.

CUTTING

Cutting is the same backward as frontward (see the section on front surfing). However, there are a few secrets to a cutting back surfer:

1. Look where you are going next. It is a much better habit to look where you are going rather than where you have been. Switch your head position at the same time you switch your paddle from one side to the other. Always be able to see the stern, even if it is out of your peripheral vision.
2. Lean your boat in the direction you want to turn. Ninty percent of the missed turns while back surfing are caused by the boater not leaning the boat in the direction he or she wants to turn. Remember, the boat wants to turn in the direction of your lean, so if you lean left and want to turn right, you will have a hard time overpowering the

boat. If you lean too much or before ruddering, you can easily catch an edge and flip. For this reason, most people don't commit to their lean.

3. Not being aware of your stern's position causes pearling, falling off the wave, and confusion. You will gain awareness through simple practice.

1. **Weight forward for park and surf.**

2. **Look at the next target.**

MOVE	**Wavespin**
WKF DEFINITION	**Treated the same as a spin in a hole. Since most rodeos are held in holes with waves, it is usually too difficult to determine whether the entire spin was done in the wave or partially in the hole. The WKF rules refer only to "spinning," with no distinction between holespinning and wavespinning.**
WKF SCORING	**1 point for each 180 degrees; .25 is added to your variety multiplier if you link a 360-degree spin. No variety points are given for a 180-degree spin.**

The wavespin is newer to playboating than the cartwheel. It is also the move that sets you free in waves. Before wavespinning, you were stuck in a forward or backward position and couldn't do anything about it. Waves were simply a surf, and possibly an ender. Now you can change from front to back and front again as often as you like, even side surfing on many waves. This move came about from the evolution of kayaks, starting with Corran Addison's Fury. The wavespin has also improved kayakers' back surfing ability, because they find themselves backward more than ever before.

To spin around on a wave, your boat must have a planing hull. Every boat planes differently, and the "looser" a boat is, the easier it is to spin. "Loose" in kayak terms means that the kayak goes from front to sideways to backward to front again with minimal resistance. Boats that are not loose drag the ends or some other part to slow the spin and drag you off the wave. On slower or smaller waves, some boats can spin easily, and others can't spin at all. You will spin much better with a loose boat.

Your goal when spinning is to get the boat end pointed downstream to slide across the water until it is pointed upstream. The end that was initially upstream will get taken downstream by the water. A kayak planes better with less weight in it. If you lean forward and put the weight in the front, the front will have more resistance in the water than the back. This is the concept of "loading and releasing." For example, if you are front surfing and want to spin backward, you want to "load" your bow and "release" your stern by leaning forward. The less weight in the end you want to slide, the better it planes. When spinning from front to back, you want your stern to plane so it can easily slide down the face of the wave into the back surf position. Your bow doesn't need to plane, since it only needs to drag up the face of the wave to swap ends with your stern. To spin from back to front, you lean backward to achieve the same load-and-release effect. The more aggressive you are at loading and releasing, the faster and more successful your spins will be.

You need to get a feel for your boat's planing characteristics. Once your boat is sideways, you must keep it planing so you don't drag off the wave. Each boat has an optimal angle (edge control) that works best when you get sideways on a wave. The flatter the boat is to the face of the wave, the better it planes. This means that you need some upstream lean. Most people have trouble committing to an upstream lean while sideways on a wave, because too much lean will cause them to power flip upstream. Practice keeping your boat as flat to the water as possible without catching your upstream edge.

Paddle position and movement. The goal for your paddle strokes is to assist the downstream end in planing upstream. Ideally, every stroke you take pushes you upstream deeper into the wave. Beginning in a front surf, rudder casually until your boat is 45 degrees to the current, then push the stern upstream as hard as you can. Use a reverse sweep with the paddle as close to the stern as possible. End your sweep when the boat is backward. Common mistakes are to start the reverse sweep while the boat is still pointed straight upstream and to start the reverse sweep too close to the center of the boat. Both mistakes cause the reverse sweep to pull the boat

downstream off the wave. Once backward, rudder the boat to 45 degrees before taking a hard forward sweep to throw the bow upstream. Since the goal of the sweep is to push the bow upstream, the sweep should start near the bow, and the paddle should push directly away from the bow. If your paddle isn't parallel to the boat and near the bow when you do your sweep, you will pull yourself off the wave.

Body position and movement. Your head and shoulders lead the spin. Make sure that you are rotated at the waist as much as possible when starting the spin. This way, your sweep has to rotate only the boat and not your body weight. When beginning the spin, throw your weight forward while keeping it centered over the boat. As soon as your boat has rotated 180 degrees, go back to the neutral position. Once you have ruddered the boat the next 45 degrees, throw your weight back to release the bow, and stay back until you have completed the spin. If you are doing only a 180-degree spin, let your body unwind as soon as you are backward and begin your back surf. If you are linking a full 360-degree turn, keep your body rotated for the full 360 degrees.

1. Let the boat turn to 45 degrees.

2. Drop your weight forward while doing a backsweep.

3. Keep rotation speed up with forward sweep and torso leading.

4. A flat boat spins best.

5. Get back in the game after the spin.

Boat position and movement. Your boat position and movement have much to do with the success of your spins, especially when linking more than one 180-degree spin at a time. Remember, during the spin process, the water is dragging your boat downstream (no matter how well you do it). This is true for most of the waves you ride. On the bigger, steeper waves, your boat actually slides down into the trough. Staying in this kind of wave is no challenge. When you are surfing a wave and contemplating spinning, you should make sure that you are near the top of the wave with some momentum toward the trough. Once you begin spinning, the current has to stop your upstream momentum before it can drag you off the wave. Usually, you can get a full 180-degree spin completed before your boat stops moving upstream. Thus, you can link another 180 before the current takes you off the wave. If you are stationary when you begin your spin, the current will immediately begin to pull you downstream and off the wave. The faster, taller, and steeper the wave, the less you need to worry about this technique. Large, steep waves will hold you on them as long as you are keeping a flat boat. Keeping the boat as flat to the wave as possible prevents the chines from digging into the water and eliminating the planing effect.

MOVE	Clean 360
WKF DEFINITION	**A clean 360 is done in the green part of the wave with one stroke where there is no foampile.**
WKF SCORING	**1 point for each 180 and a bonus point for being clean; .5 is added to your variety multiplier.**

The technique for one-stroke 360s (or more) is identical to the technique for a normal wavespin. The only difference is that both your technique and the wave must be better than those necessary to succeed in a two-stroke 360. Except on really steep, tall, fast waves, you must have as much upstream momentum as possible when you begin your spin. The second 180 will be much slower using no strokes, so the water has more time to pull you off the wave. Your body motion has to be very effective for loading and releasing the second 180. Generally, when people do 540s or more, they are simply loading and releasing the ends (by shifting their weight forward and back). On a really good wave, it is possible to spin endlessly using only your body weight and boat leans. Controlling your boat without a paddle is a good exercise to practice. You learn the boat's capabilities, as well as how to make boat leans and weight shifts do most of the work you have been doing with the paddle. Many people who can do wavespins use only full power with their paddle strokes. They never get a feel for the minimal effort needed or what the boat can do with a softer touch. Practicing one-stroke 360s and spinning without any strokes will improve your spinning technique and boat control.

Paddle position and movement. Anywhere but in the water.

Body position and movement. See wavespinning body position.

Boat position and movement. The keys to spinning more than 360 degrees without a stroke are as follows:

1. Start with a wave you can side surf (steep, fast, big).
2. Get the boat started with a one-stroke 360.
3. Load and release the ends after they are 45 degrees off the current. You may need to drop your downstream edge the moment you load the end to get the current to drag your end downstream. Your boat can get stuck in the side-surf position. Loading the end you want to go downstream and dropping your downstream edge can also get you out of that position.
4. The most difficult part of spinning with no paddle occurs the moment your boat is parallel to the current and wants to lock into a front surf or back surf. Loading and releasing in this position will not help you break out of the surf. Just before you are straight, lean the boat in the direction you want it to go until it comes around another 45 degrees; then you can load and release again. Repeat for more.

1. Begin the spin with gusto.

2. Keep the boat flat.

3. Finish the initial stroke.

4. Keep your head and body leading, weight slightly back.

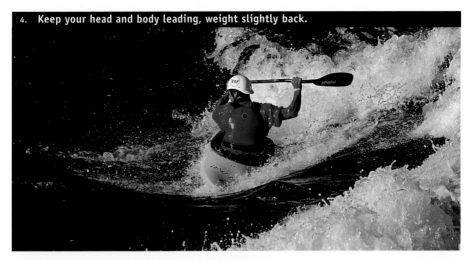

5. Enjoy the ride.

6. Finish in surf position.

MOVE	**Blunt**
WKF DEFINITION	An elevated wave move done in the green part of the wave against the grain. It must be elevated beyond 45 degrees and done on the shoulder of the wave or a hole. The spin direction must bring the bow toward the center of the wave for a front blunt, or bring the stern toward the center for a stern blunt (against the grain).
WKF SCORING	The blunt is treated like a 180-degree direction change and scores 2 points for 45- to 70-degree elevation or 4 points for 71- to 110-degree elevation; .75 is added to your variety multiplier.

The blunt is a fancy way of doing an aggressive cutback and an elevated wavespin at the same time. It is a very dynamic looking move, and it gives boaters another way to cut back at the end of a wave or next to a hole. The breakdown of a blunt is as follows;

1. Do an aggressive cut to the side of the wave or past the corner of a hole.
2. Begin an aggressive cutback, but drop your upstream edge more than you would for a normal cutback while simultaneously initiating the bow into the water at the 12 o'clock position.
3. Continue to bring the bow through the water until you are in the back surf position. Then flatten the boat out so you can drop into a back surf. You have essentially done a retendo on a wave.

Paddle position and movement

1. After you have done an aggressive cut over to the edge of the wave, have your paddle in the water in rudder position.
2. Begin the blunt by ruddering the boat back from 45 degrees to straight upstream at 12 o'clock.
3. The paddle should now be perpendicular to the boat, and you should be initiating the bow in the water with a strong backsweep starting at your hip. The paddle starts at your stern for the rudder, then it is converted to a backsweep-initiation stroke at your hip.
4. Follow up the initiation stroke with a backstroke on the opposite side of the boat to keep yourself on the wave. You should be back surfing now.

Body position and movement. Your body position and movement are identical to the Ollie (see later in this chapter). Keep your body in the neutral position until you are in position to blunt. Then lean back hard while lifting the knees to raise the bow. Immediately throw your weight forward and begin your initiation stroke. This body motion gets the boat free of the water and gives you some rotational speed before you do your stroke. The end result is a faster, highter, more retentive blunt.

Boat position and movement

1. The boat should start on the shoulder of the wave, pointed about 45 degrees away from the center of the wave.

2. At the moment you begin your blunt, you should have speed down the wave. The more speed you have upstream, the less likely that you will fall off the back of the wave after you have completed your blunt.

3. It helps to "Ollie" the boat a little before doing the blunt. This is simply lifting the bow up and then throwing it down quickly. You do this with body movement. It helps you get more rotational speed with the boat. This makes the blunt more impressive looking and also makes it more likely that you will stay on the wave.

4. When you begin your rudder and backsweep, you are watching your bow. At the moment it is pointed straight upstream (12 o'clock), you can drop your edge (if you are spinning left, drop your left edge) into the water at an angle of your choosing. The angle at which you drop your edge is the same angle that your boat will elevate. When learning the blunt, drop your edge 45 degrees, which is the minimum necessary. When doing the backsweep, you want to pull the bow downstream as fast as you can so that you will be able to drop into a back surf before you fall off the wave. The entire process of being elevated should take less than a second.

5. Your boat will drop into a back surf position and surf you back into the center of the wave.

1. Begin an aggressive cutback when you reach top speed.

2. Drop lots of edge and initiate hard to get the boat vertical quickly without flushing.

3. Speed on the way into the move helps you throw a nice spray.

4. Throw in a backstroke and flatten out the boat when you sit back down.

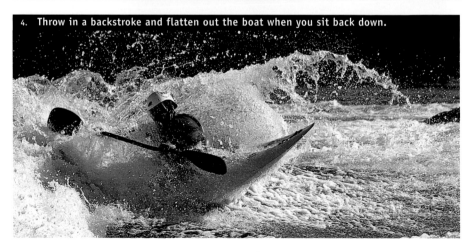

MOVE	Shuvit
WKF DEFINITION	A 180-degree wavespin followed by an immediate reverse of direction for another 180-degree wavespin back to where you started. A shuvit can be done in a wave or hole, flat or elevated.
WKF SCORING	Scored the same as all 180-degree changes in direction: 1 point for less than 45 degrees, 2 points for 45 to 70 degrees, and 4 points for 71 to 110 degrees (if both 180s are more than 70 degrees, it is a splitwheel, not a shuvit); .5 is added to your variety multiplier.

A shuvit is a great way to start a move and then change direction. It gives you some margin for error when trying splitwheels and not getting vertical enough (at least you get something). Plus, they are really fun.

Paddle position and movement. The paddle position and movement are identical to a 360-degree wavespin, except you do the entire move with one blade. You spin from the front surf to the back surf with a reverse sweep (see wavespin technique), then convert that reverse sweep into a forward sweep once you are backward, and spin the boat back into a front surf (see wavespin for the back-to-front part of the spin).

Body position and movement. Your body is the same as in a wavespin. Lead the spin with your head and body; then

1. Begin the spin.

load and release. When backward, rotate your head and body to spin in the opposite direction; then load and release.

Boat position and movement. A shuvit requires the boat to spin a full 180 degrees from front to back, and then from back to front. When trying the shuvit, most people don't spin the full 180 degrees each way. Do not stop spinning until you complete the first 180-degree rotation; then

start spinning the other way. Your boat position and movement are the same as in a wavespin, or two 180s linked together.

ELEVATED SHUVITS

If you are in a hole or steep wave, it is possible to elevate your shuvits. This means that you are trying to do splitwheels without going totally vertical (see the description of splitwheels in chapter 8).

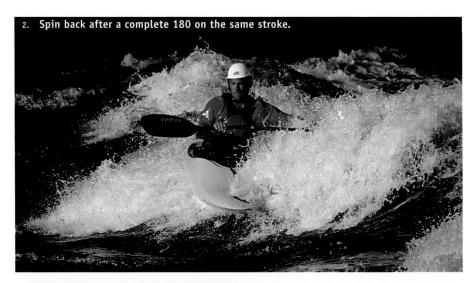
2. Spin back after a complete 180 on the same stroke.

3. Finish in original position.

MOVE	Wavewheel
WKF DEFINITION	**A vertical cartwheel over the top of a wave while paddling downstream.**
WKF SCORING	**Scored the same as all direction changes, except that no points are given for an elevation under 45 degrees. It is either elevated or vertical (2 or 4 points), with .5 added to your variety multiplier.**

Wavewheels have changed the way playboaters run a river more than any other move. Before wavewheels, playboaters would spend most of their time trying to catch and surf every wave possible. Now, you see playboaters giving up many great surfing waves to do flying wavewheels over the waves instead. Some will tell you about the wavewheel they should have skipped due to the ugly rock behind the wave, or about pitoning the bottom of the river because it was too shallow. Having said that, wavewheels are as safe as any playboating move, if you know the river.

The wavewheel is a cartwheel that uses the peak of a wave to make the cartwheel possible. The move is a leap off the peak of a wave, followed by an instantaneous rotating of the boat to get as vertical as possible before the bow hits the water. Once the bow hits the water, you pull it under you as if you were cartwheeling. With good technique and the right boat, a wavewheel takes very little physical effort. Lack of strength is not why most wavewheels fail, but as with almost any physical activity, strength doesn't hurt.

Paddle position and movement. The wavewheel is a combination of a forward stroke off the peak of a wave into an initiation stroke immediately after leaving the peak of the wave. This gives you your first end. Do a stern initiation stroke to slam the stern for end number two. This doesn't require much timing with the waves. Timing of the forward stroke and the bow initiation stroke, along with boat position, are key to whether you will get the boat vertical or not and achieve a wavewheel.

Spot the wave, about 2 feet high. Start paddling toward it at a medium pace. Aim for the peak of the wave, where there is no break. As your boat reaches the trough, plant your paddle in the wave about halfway up. Pull hard to get your body to leap off the peak, then snap, and convert your forward stroke into an initia-tion stroke. Lean way forward, and drop your edge about 75 degrees, trying to get the boat vertical before it hits the water. Since the bow hits the water before the boat is vertical, continue to pull the bow under you with a strong finish to your initiation stroke. Once you get vertical, stand on your footpegs and look around, because the air is nice up there. This is a typical wavewheel.

The goal for your chosen wave is to pull your body just off the peak of the wave with a forward stroke. This means that your body will go a little higher than the peak of the wave, and your bow will be higher than the peak. Most people try to pull the stern under the water by leaning the boat on edge and sweeping up the wave like a rocket move. This makes it very difficult to snap the boat back down again.

Body position and movement. Keep your body neutral and over the boat until you begin the bow initiation stroke. Throw your body forward so that all your weight goes into helping slice the bow under the water while you complete the initiation stroke. Once you are vertical, you can stand up and look around or complete your second end of the wavewheel by keeping your body neutral during the stern initiation stroke. Your ability to do eddyline or flatwater cartwheels is a good measure of your ability to wavewheel.

Boat position and movement. Keep your boat riding up the face of the wave at the same angle as the face of the wave. If the wave has a face that is a 45-degree angle, your boat should be at a 45-degree angle to the sky. Don't pull the stern under the water. Once you begin to snap the bow down, put your edge down at 75 degrees (plus or minus 10 degrees). As soon as the boat is nearly vertical, it should be 90 degrees on edge so the deck is facing one bank and the hull the other. After you are vertical, you have many options. Slam the stern, splitwheel, pirouette, or bring the boat down the way it came up and continue down the river. The most common move is to slam the stern. This is done by switching to the stern initiation stroke and doing a very hard forward sweep, while keeping the boat on edge.

1. Lining up.

2. Begin pull and lean.

3. Finish pull off the wave.

5. Finish the initiation stroke; lean back to stall.

4. Begin the initiation stroke and increase your lean.

6. Slam the stern.

7. Finish the stern initiation stroke.

9. Go on your way.

8. Look at the target and bring your bow down.

MOVE	Stern Wavewheel
WKF DEFINITION	**Same as wavewheel.**
WKF SCORING	**Same as wavewheel.**

D oing a wavewheel backward to initiate the stern instead of the bow is not much more difficult. It is more difficult to see where you are going, but the move itself is about the same. Everything you learned about a wavewheel applies for the stern wavewheel.

Paddle position and movement. Paddle backward to the wave; use a backstroke up the face of the wave and a stern initiation stroke after you reach the peak.

Body position and movement. When lining up for a wave to do a stern wavewheel, it is best to come down on the wave a little sideways so you can keep your eye on the wave. As you reach the peak of the wave, drop your weight back to make it easier to initiate the stern.

Boat position and movement. As soon as you are in the trough of the wave, straighten the boat out and push yourself off the peak of the wave. Initiate the stern as soon as you feel yourself leaving the peak of the wave. Your boat should go vertical. Try not to go past vertical unless you know that there are no rocks downstream. It is easy to tip over on a stern wavewheel.

45

MOVE	Kickflip
WKF DEFINITION	A barrel roll done after paddling downstream off the peak of a wave. Must be done without the body touching the water.
WKF SCORING	6 points technical; 1 point is added to your variety multiplier.

Wilderness Tours on the Ottawa has a kayaker in a slalom boat doing a kickflip off Baby Face wave on its promotional video from 1995. That is where I first saw it. It is done exactly the same as a wavewheel until you leave the peak of the wave. Once you pull yourself off the peak of the wave, you tuck and roll in the air. It requires using your paddle to make the boat do the flip before you land on the water again. The easiest place to learn kickflips is in the ocean, where you can catch some big air paddling out through the waves.

Paddle position and movement. Paddle up to a big wave with no break as fast as you can. Pull yourself up the face of the wave like a wavewheel. After you leave the peak of the wave, reach as far under the boat with an initiation stroke as you can. Pirouette the boat upside down while tucked forward by using your initiation stroke, but instead of initiating the bow, roll the boat on top of you. As soon as you are upside down, switch to an eskimo rolling stroke on the other side and do a quick slap roll before you hit the water. You should land right side up.

Body position and movement. Start in the neutral position. As you leave the wave, tuck forward to get the bow to come down and to reach the water with your paddle. As soon as you are upside down, lean back to finish the roll.

Boat position and movement. As you leave the peak of the wave, roll your boat in the air and land upright.

1. Pull up the wave with speed.

2. Throw your body in the direction of the flip.

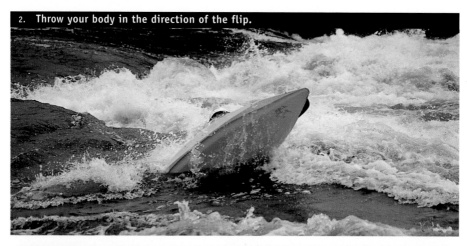

3. Bring your body and paddle under boat.

4. Sweep your body on top of the boat and continue on your way.

MOVE	Grinding
WKF DEFINITION	Side surfing the green part of a wave for three seconds.
WKF SCORING	2 points technical; .25 is added to your variety multiplier.

Grinding waves is a terrific feeling. You get the sensation of the ultimate slide. It is generally very smooth (as smooth as the wave), and you can do all kinds of great tricks. Grinding is only for boats with planing hulls. The better the hull, the more waves you can grind.

To start the grind, front surf the wave of choice (it must be at least 2 feet high, have 45 degrees or more of face angle, and be fast). Begin a wavespin, but stop the spin when you are sideways. Do this by pulling forward on your paddle immediately after doing the reverse sweep, spin stroke. Hold the boat sideways with your downstream paddle by doing forward sweeps when the bow rises up the wave, or reverse sweeps when the stern rises up the wave. Drop your upstream edge so the boat is as flat on the water as possible without catching the upstream edge. Now sit and enjoy. It is very similar to the feeling of sliding down a snow-covered hill sideways in a kayak. The boat is tipped downhill, and you control the boat with your paddle the same way.

Paddle position and movement. The paddle is not really needed during grinding, but keep it ready to stop the boat from traveling unnecessarily.

Body position and movement. Keep your body weight completely centered over the center of the boat—front to back and side to side. Controlling the boat requires small weight shifts front or back. If the bow is sliding down the wave, lean forward to load the bow and release the stern, and lean back to stop the stern from sliding.

Boat position and movement. Start with the boat on top of the wave near the peak. Spin sideways while near the top. This is where the wave is steepest and will likely hold your grind. Hold the boat as flat to the water as you can without catching the upstream edge. Watch the oncoming water and keep your upstream edge half an inch off the water.

To make your boat skip and jump out of the water:
- Drop your upstream edge into the water until it catches, water loads up on the side, and you begin to travel up the wave.
- As soon as you get near the top, but before you lose your balance, flatten the boat out again and hop up on your butt.
- Enjoy this moment of air as you land and slide back down the wave, or roll up because you power flipped.

1. **Begin your spin at the top of the wave.**

2. **Grind to the bottom of the wave, holding the boat angled sideways to the wave.**

MOVE	**Ender**
WKF DEFINITION	**Any single end that is elevated more than 45 degrees. (This definition was created to give one-end moves a way to be scored. It is a much broader definition than what most kayakers think of when imagining an ender. We will learn how to do the old-style up-and-over enders.)**
WKF SCORING	**2 points for 45 to 70 degrees, 4 points for 71 to 110 degrees (vertical); .5 is added to your variety multiplier.**

Enders are the tricks of the original kayak heroes. The ability to stand a 4-meter, 80-gallon kayak on end took skill. You would fly so high that you couldn't reach the water with your paddle, and sometimes it even hurt when your face slapped the water on landing. Where I come from, we were so obsessed with enders that we would measure how good the day was by counting the number of enders (500 was not an unusual number).

Now enders can be done in flatwater with the right boat and technique. The move doesn't have the thrill of the launch into orbit and crash back to earth that it used to, because of the size of the boats we paddle today. They are still worth obsessing over, however, until you can cartwheel; then you can obsess over cartwheels.

Doing enders is simply a matter of finding a way to get your bow or stern under the water using the oncoming water in a wave. Many waves aren't steep enough to guarantee you an ender, and many boats are designed to prevent the bow or stern from going under. This means that you need a technique to ensure that you can get enders when you want them, instead of when the conditions are perfect.

Start by surfing a wave and finding the deepest, steepest part of it. This is the sweet spot for enders. Get to the top of the wave and back to the sweet spot. Take a hard forward stroke to get the boat moving back into the trough of the wave. Lean forward to seesaw your bow down as much as possible before it hits the water. As soon as your bow hits the water, keep the boat flat and straight and your weight forward until you are almost completely vertical. Once you are almost vertical, throw your weight toward the sky and stand on your footbraces. This is an ender. If you want to go higher, you need to turn your rudder into a strong backstroke as soon as the boat is elevated 45 degrees and until you are vertical. This strong backstroke can also be converted into a pirouetting stroke.

A back ender is the same as a front ender, but the stern goes under the water and the bow goes in the air. In competition, there is no distinction between them. A back ender on a wave is easier, in that you can get the stern down more easily on most boats because it is usually smaller and you can throw your weight back easily. Use the same technique for front enders, except in reverse. If you have a planing-hulled boat, it is easier to spin on a wave first and then do a back ender.

Paddle position and movement. Begin with a forward stroke when the boat is completely on the top of the wave. This causes the boat to start dropping into the sweet spot. Convert the forward stroke into a rudder to keep the boat straight until the boat is elevated 45 degrees. Convert the rudder into a strong backstroke to help give you more height.

Body position and movement. Your body should be in a neutral position until you are ready to seesaw the boat down. At the moment you take your forward stroke, throw your weight forward and keep it there until the boat is almost vertical.

Then throw your weight to the sky to get extra height and a better view and to be in position to pirouette.

Boat position and movement. The boat should start at the peak of the wave. Your rudder keeps the boat perfectly straight to the oncoming water. Your ends should be out of the water and ready to seesaw the bow down. This is where most people make mistakes. They let the boat start to surf down to the trough, where the wave may not be steep enough to ender them. (It is important to drop the bow as much as possible, getting the boat as vertical as possible before the bow touches the water.) After the bow starts going under the water, it is critical to keep the boat straight and flat until you are almost vertical.

A nice ender always feels good. Bring your body onto the back deck and stand on the footbraces as soon as the boat is vertical.

MOVE	Pirouette
WKF DEFINITION	360-degree spin of the kayak in the vertical plane; rotating the boat while vertical.
WKF SCORING	2 technical points; .5 is added to your variety multiplier.

In the progression of playboating, the pirouette was the second major development. In 1979, most people were getting 180-degree pirouettes, but very few people were getting 360s. During the 1980s, it was the 360-degree pirouette that set the best playboaters apart from the rest. Getting a big booming ender with a 360- to 540-degree pirouette off one stroke while totally vertical was a big accomplishment. Many people were beginning to get pirouettes of 360 degrees or more on corner holes, but very few could pirouette more than 180 degrees. Now people are learning to get pirouettes their first year kayaking. Getting a pirouette requires that you get vertical in your kayak first. Pirouettes are discussed here in the context of endering in a wave.

Paddle position and movement. Once you are almost vertical and you have done a backstroke to push you higher, convert your backstroke into a pushing stroke across your bow. If, for example, you are doing a final rudder and backstroke on the left during your ender, you take your left blade and push it in front of your bow toward the right side of the boat. Remember that you are vertical, so your blade will be in the water when it is over the deck. Once you have pushed the paddle as far as you can, leave it there until you hit the water.

Body position and movement. With every turn you do, you want to look in the direction you are rotating as well as turn your shoulders that way. Once you begin to push the paddle in front of your bow (the pirouetting stroke), you should throw your head and body in the direction you want to rotate. This throw will pirouette the boat along with the stroke and give you the potential for a full 360.

Boat position and movement. The boat will rotate on end. You must be vertical to pirouette easily. If you begin the pirouette before you are vertical, you will not get vertical. The water will shed off the deck, and you will begin to fall back down.

MOVE	Wave Loop
WKF DEFINITION	An ender that shoots the boat completely airborne with a 180-degree flip so that the boat lands on the stern and falls back into the front-surfing position. It doesn't have to be retentive.
WKF SCORING	4 points for each end and a 6-point bonus for the flip; 1.5 is added to your variety multiplier.

There are very few people in very few places getting loops on waves. It requires a boat that can get some air on an ender, a wave that is very fast and has a pocket that will shoot you high, and the ability to tuck and flip in the air. I am listing the move here because it is very exciting and I hope that more people will start trying it.

To do a loop, you need a wave that is fast and flat in the trough, steep at the top, and as long as your boat. Your boat should have little rocker and enough volume to get you airborne.

Paddle position and movement. Your goal when doing a wave loop is to get the maximum height possible during the ender part of the loop. To get maximum height, convert the rudder you are using to keep the boat straight into a backstroke as soon as the boat begins to ender. Push as hard as possible on that backstroke to assist the water in shooting you upward. Keep pushing yourself up in the air until you can't reach the water with your paddle anymore. That is the moment you will begin your flip. If you have to do the cheating stroke to finish the flip, it is simply a hard forward sweep on the downstream side, pulling the stern through the water so that the stern will be downstream of the bow.

Body position and movement. You use your body weight to make the boat do a flip in the air and get extra height. When you set up the ender, your body starts out in the forward position. Once the bow is submerged, begin your backstroke and bring your body backward, as if to throw your weight to the sky. You are also trying to get the boat past vertical with this body weight throw. Time it so that your body is perpendicular to the boat at the moment the boat is vertical, so that your weight is trying to tip the boat forward. From that moment on, when you throw your weight backward, you will actually be throwing it slightly upstream and upward. The moment you have your body against the back deck and the boat is as high as it is going to go, tuck as hard and quickly as you can back into the forward position. This will flip the boat in the air so the stern comes around and lands in the water first. When your stern hits the water, it is usually not around enough to land you upright, so you can cheat a little. Rotate the boat sideways with your hip tilt so that when the stern hits you can sweep the stern through the water. This allows you to get the stern downstream of the bow so that you can land right side up.

Boat position and movement. Your boat starts out in the normal ender position, with an emphasis on starting high on the wave and dropping into the trough with speed. Keep the boat flat and straight during the ender part, and try to get as much momentum as possible for the flip upward. When flipping, try to keep the boat flat so that it will look like a flip instead of some kind of barrel roll.

MOVE	**Ollie**
WKF DEFINITION	**While front or back surfing a wave, doing a 180-degree spin in the air. The boat must be completely out of the water.**
WKF SCORING	**A 4-point bonus is added to the normal 1-point technical score for a 180-degree spin; .75 is added to your variety multiplier.**

Ollies became possible when planing hulls were put on kayaks. The move is a bounce into the air using body motions on a fast, steep wave. Next, the boat is spun lightning quick 180 degrees before it lands in the water again. It is usually done from the front-surf position, landing in the back-surf position.

Paddle position and movement. You can have the paddle in the air when starting the Ollie. Use a super-quick reverse sweep to rotate the boat 180 degrees as soon as it is almost airborne. Carry your sweep all the way to the bow so that you will have a rudder to surf with when you are done with the Ollie.

Body position and movement. Start with your body in the neutral position. As soon as you are halfway down the wave, throw your torso back and lift hard on your knees to get the bow up in the air. As soon as the bow is in the air, throw your torso back into the neutral position and let your knees drop down. This will make the boat hop. To make the 180-degree spin, you must have your head and body rotated in the direction you want to turn when you take the reverse sweep.

Boat position and movement. You start the Ollie high up on the wave and shooting down the face with speed. As soon as you are halfway down the face of the wave, make the bow jump high into the air by leaning back hard and lifting your knees. As soon as the bow jumps up high, throw it back down and spin the boat at the same time. Lifting the bow gets your body out of the water. When you throw the bow back down, the stern lifts out of the water, and your body is still out of the water. You must rotate the boat 180 degrees during the brief moment you are in the air. Anybody who rides a skateboard or can do bunny-hops on a bicycle will understand the principle being used for the Ollie.

CHAPTER EIGHT

Hole Moves

Hole riding is not new to kayaking by any means. Kayakers have been putting themselves in holes from the very beginning of the sport. New shorter and higher-performance boats have helped to transform hole riding from side-surfing endurance contests to incredible "expression sessions" where the kayak never stops doing something exciting. Holes have an attraction that is addictive and multifaceted. There is the excitement factor of never knowing what is going to happen next. I still don't know a single kayaker in the world who surfs holes and never gets out of control. Sticking yourself in the middle of a 1 million horsepower washing machine can be unpredictable at times. It's not the potential for danger that makes it exciting, just the fact that you are not in total control.

The feel of the water is an incredible lure. The water rushing under your boat and the backwash pulsing around your body is a feel you don't get anywhere else in any other sport. It is as intimate as you can get with the river and stay in your boat. The river is incredibly alive in a hole—pulsing, pushing, pulling—and you are held there as if the river wants you there. There is the lure of learning to master a hole that keeps you coming back. Hole riding is incredibly fun as a beginner, and it only gets better after that. Most playboaters are addicted to holes, and they spend most of their time surfing them.

Hole riding is incredibly rewarding once the basic moves become fairly easy for you. There is so much you can do in a hole that it is almost impossible to get bored with one, unless you have a limited imagination.

When I discuss holes I am referring to both pourover holes and wave holes—any hole that has a backwash and you can side surf.

MOVE	Spin
WKF DEFINITION	A 360-degree linked spin in a hole done at an elevation less than 45 degrees.
WKF SCORING	1 point for each 180-degree direction change (2 points total for a 360-degree spin); .25 is added to your variety multiplier.

Because new boat designs include planing hulls and lower-volume, slicier ends, it is now possible to spin anywhere in most holes. In the past, spinning was possible only on the corners of holes due to boat design limitations.

Spinning is ultimately the most critical move for hole surfing because it is the easiest way to turn around or set up a different move. I offer the techniques for spinning both on corners and in the middle of a hole.

SPINNING ON THE CORNER OF A HOLE

Spinning on the corner of a hole is easy because one end of the boat will naturally get swept downstream if it is sticking out past the corner. The other end of the kayak stays in the hole so you don't wash out of the hole. The technique involves three factors: using forward and backsweeps to keep the boat spinning, keeping your body over the corner of the hole, and keeping the ends of the kayak out of the water.

Paddle position and movement. Paddle strokes are used to rotate the boat in a circle using a combination of forward and backsweeps, as if you were trying to spin in circles in flatwater. The other objective of the paddle strokes is to keep your body on the corner of the hole so you don't wash out or fall deep into the hole. Let's start off by pretending that you are side surfing a hole with your right side downstream. Pull yourself forward to the corner with a combination high brace–forward stroke. As soon as the bow starts to get swept downstream, you need to pull your body out to the corner of the hole with a little more power in your for-

ward stroke–high brace combination. You will be spinning to the right, so look at the stern over your right shoulder. As soon as the stern is clear of the oncoming water, take your right blade out of the water and put your left one in the water in a forward sweep position. Quickly sweep the boat to the right so that you are facing upstream. As soon as you are almost completely facing upstream, switch from the front sweep on the left to a backsweep on the right. You have just done a 360-degree spin on the corner of a hole.

Body position and movement. Stay in a neutral position and lead the spin with your head and body. Keep your body on the corner of the hole. When you are doing your sweeps, monitor your body position to see that you are not getting swept out of the hole or deep into it. Adjust your strokes to hold your body on the corner.

Boat position and movement. Keep the boat as flat as possible when spinning. If you lean downstream too much, your boat will want to surf out of the hole, and you will be less likely to stay in the hole when you spin.

SPINNING IN THE MIDDLE OF A HOLE

Spinning in the middle of a hole is actually the same technique as wavespinning. It takes more energy because the foampile slows down the boat. The flatter the hole, the easier it is to spin. Pourovers are not easy to spin; in fact, those are called blast-wheels.

Paddle position and movement. Same as a wavespin.

Body position and movement. Same as a wavespin.

Boat position and movement. You need to begin by blasting the hole or by surfing down and in front of the foampile before starting to spin. The entire spin is done with the boat surfing in the trough of the hole, not on top of the foampile. The key to spinning in a hole is to not give up on your strokes until the boat has completely spun either frontward or backward into the blasting position. Also, the load-and-release technique really helps.

1. Begin moving to the corner of the hole.

2. Pull your body to the corner of the hole using a high brace/forward stroke combination.

3. Keep the boat flat to oncoming water, lead with your head and body, and forward sweep from backward to front position.

4. Once forward, you can keep going or do something else.

MOVE	Retendo
WKF DEFINITION	Retendos fall under the ender category in international competition.
WKF SCORING	See Ender.

DOING VERTICAL MOVES IN HOLES

There are many different kinds of holes that you can do rentendos and cartwheels in. Each hole has its own characteristics that you must adjust for. Learn everthing you can about holes before trying vertical moves in them. Following is a list of questions you need to ask yourself about a hole.

1. *Retentiveness:* How strong is the foampile of the hole? You can tell how "retentive" a hole is by how much water comes back upstream. Many tall holes aren't retentive because the water just falls straight down into the trough of the hole instead of rushing upstream. Where is it the strongest? All holes have weak spots and strong spots. You are almost always looking for the strong spot. That area could be only a foot wide on smaller holes.

2. *Deepness:* Is the water deep enough, or is there a deep spot where you can go vertical? If the river is wide and shallow, the hole may not be deep enough to get vertical in. Look for where the river is constricted and deep. If you can see the rock that makes the hole, you can see how deep it is. The hole usually needs to be about 3 to 4 feet deep to do retendos and cartwheels (depending on your boat and how much you weigh). Holes usually contain places that are deep and shallow as well. The deep spots tend to be on the corners where the rock ends.

3. *Sidedness:* Is it a righty or lefty hole? Or can you go either way? Almost every hole favors dropping either your right edge or your left edge. As you are facing upstream in a hole, if the hole is deeper, stronger, or more retentive to the left side, it is probably a lefty hole (and vice versa for righty holes). If the hole is fairly symmetrical and deep everywhere, you can probably go in either direction.

The controlled retendo was the start of hole riding as we know it today. The ability to go vertical in a hole and not flush out is what gives hole riding so much appeal. It gives you the opportunity to extend a ride beyond one move. I approach retendos as if you were planning to learn cartwheels next. There are many ways to ender in a hole and not flush out. Here we stick to the cartwheel technique so that you can use retendos to build on what you have learned.

Most rodeo boats are "slicier" edgewise than top to bottom. This means that water flows around the kayak with less drag if it is hitting the edge of the kayak than if it is hitting the deck of the kayak (like an ender). Staying in a hole involves keeping the forces that are holding you in the hole equal to or greater than the forces pushing you out of the hole. The main force pushing you out of a hole during retendos and cartwheels is the force of the oncoming water against the kayak when it is vertical. This is one reason why retendos and cartwheels are done with the boat on edge instead of flat, like enders. Being able to lean your boat on either edge, on demand, and keep your balance while initiating are mandatory skills for cartwheeling and make retendos much easier as well.

Paddle position and movement. Your paddle's primary function is to get the bow down at precisely the right time and at the right angle. If the hole isn't very strong, the other function of your paddle stroke is to stay retentive. When doing the initiation stroke, try to keep the left blade flat on the top of the foampile. This position lifts the stern and helps sink the bow, but it doesn't push you backward out of the hole. If the hole is very strong, you will want to "hold back" on the hole. To do this, keep the initiation stroke very vertical so that you can push yourself downstream and prevent yourself from being thrown too deep into the hole. Your paddle strokes are trying to either keep you in the hole (90 percent of the time) or hold back on the hole (5 percent of the time); the other 5 percent of the time, they don't need to do either because of perfect equilibrium.

Body position and movement. Your body is neutral when setting up the retendo. As soon as you begin the initiation stroke, throw your weight forward to help get the bow down. Bring your body back to neutral as soon as the boat is nearly vertical. The entire time, try to keep your weight over the boat and your butt firmly on the seat. Don't throw your body around; in particular, don't throw it off to the side. As long as your weight stays over the center of the boat, retendos and cartwheels will be easy to balance.

Boat position and movement. There a thousand ways to get into position to do a retendo. Here I discuss the most common way of setting it up. Ferry out to the hole and get lined up at the most retentive and deepest spot available. You should be in a front-surf position, and your body should be near the top of the foampile. If you aren't sure where the good spot is, watch somebody who is doing well in the hole. Once in position, let your boat begin to drop into the trough of the hole. As soon as you have forward momentum toward the trough, lean the boat on the

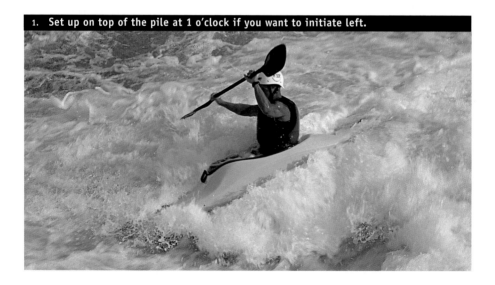

1. Set up on top of the pile at 1 o'clock if you want to initiate left.

2. Initiate at 12 o'clock, standing on footbraces if you want to go higher.

3. Get your weight back to neutral and finish with the second part of a spin to keep from back endering.

edge toward the side of the hole that is deepest or toward the closest corner. You should lean the boat about 45 degrees while learning. Keep the boat pointed straight upstream until it hits the oncoming water. Using your initiation stroke at the moment the bow hits the water, try to submerge the bow and throw the stern upstream. If you had a 45-degree lean, your boat will not go totally vertical. The more edge you drop, the more vertical you go. If your bow hits at 12 o'clock,

you will go more vertical than if it hits at 11 o'clock (assuming you are initiating to the left). Using the numbers on a clock helps to communicate to other boaters what angle you are initiating at. Generally, it is best to initiate between 10 and 2 o'clock, with 12 o'clock being the easiest.

There are two things that happen when you are learning retendos that can be frustrating. The first is that the boat never goes vertical; instead, the bow just gets swept off to the side and you end up side surfing again. This is caused by initiating at 10 o'clock instead of 12. Often you try to initiate at 12 o'clock but start the initiation stroke too early; by the time the bow actually hits the water, it is at 10 o'clock and the current simply pushes the bow off to the side instead of under the water. Another reason that the bow doesn't go under water is that you didn't have enough dropped edge. This causes the initiation stroke to rotate the boat to the left instead of down into the water. The other common mistake is dropping too much edge (leaning the boat on edge too much), initiating at 1 o'clock instead of 12 o'clock, and having the water flip you over upstream. This is easily fixed by initiating at 12 or 11 o'clock and not dropping so much edge.

Assuming that the bow went under and you are getting vertical, you still need to stay in the hole. A strong hole will automatically hold you in. In that case, you are just trying to sit the kayak back down in the water in a side surf so that you can start over. The best way to do that is to switch from the initiation stroke on the left to the right paddle blade immediately when the boat is vertical. Do a forward sweep with the right blade to bring the stern around to upstream and down in a side-surf position (surfing with your right blade downstream). The reason to bring the boat around to this position is because it is the first step to cartwheeling. A weaker hole requires that when you switch to your right blade you begin taking a strong backstroke, which will push you upstream and keep you from flushing out of the hole.

INITIATING THE STERN FOR RETENDOS

The stern initiation for retendos is as fun and as important to future moves as the bow initiation. Remember that cartwheels are both stern and bow initiations. Setting up a stern initiation is different because it is more difficult to back surf out to the hole and set up on top of the foampile backward. Instead, try starting in a side-surf position and pull yourself to the corner you want to do the retendo on (for purposes of this discussion, the left corner as you look upstream). Once you are at the corner and the bow is almost straight downstream, you are ready to begin a stern-initiated retendo.

Paddle position and movement. You have the left blade in the water as you pull yourself to the edge of the hole and get your bow downstream. Your paddle should be in the closed-faced bow draw position to help pull the bow down. The closed-faced position will help surf you back toward the center of the hole. As soon as your body is high enough out of the hole so the stern is clear of the oncoming water, switch to the right blade and pull the stern around to 12 o'clock. Once at 12 o'clock, do the stern initiation stroke (a forward sweep). If the hole is strong, you can sweep hard without worrying about pulling yourself out of the hole. If it is weak, you need to keep the paddle as flat to the surface of the water as possible. This means keeping your right arm high and your left arm down low by your side. This way, you are sweeping the bow upstream instead of the stern downstream. Once the bow is overhead and coming back down, switch to a forward stroke on the left to keep you in the hole.

Body position and movement. When you surf to the corner of the hole, make sure that you are looking to the left to see the stern and where it is relative to the oncoming water. This means rotating your body in the direction you are about to turn. Keep your body in a neutral position

1. **Begin looking back over your upstream shoulder to set up.**

2. **Drop the edge to 45-plus degrees and begin a forward sweep.**

during the initiation stroke. Leaning back during the stern initiation causes all kinds of problems, especially when cartwheeling. Keep your weight over the boat.

Boat position and movement. Once the boat is pointed almost straight downstream, the stern should be just about hitting the oncoming water and still be angled at 1 o'clock. You switch to your right blade, do the initiation stroke to get the boat to 12 o'clock, and drop your edge 45 degrees. It is identical to the bow-initiated retendo except that you are hitting the stern. Bring the bow all the way up and around to the front-surf position before flattening it out again. The difficulty with stern-initiated cartwheels is getting into position with enough of the boat in the hole to stay retentive. Often when you surf out to the corner and then initiate the stern, you are too far past the strong part of the hole and just wash out.

3. **Keep your weight forward, using your edge to control elevation.**

4. Switch to a forward stroke on the other side when the boat is vertical.

6. Flatten the boat out once you are nearly horizontal again.

5. Continue to pull on forward stroke to keep yourself in the hole.

7. Back on top of the foampile.

MOVE	Cartwheel
WKF DEFINITION	Two linked ends, each elevated past 45 degrees. "Linked" means no more than one stroke or three seconds between ends.
WKF SCORING	Each end scores 2 points for 45 to 70 degrees of elevation or 4 points for 71 to 110 degrees of elevation; .75 is added to your variety multiplier for both left- and right-initiated cartwheels.

Cartwheeling is a game of equilibrium, the ultimate challenge of balance, wits, and adaptability. Cartwheels are a three-dimensional move with every axis in play at once. You have the x-axis, where your goal is to stay in the sweet spot of the hole. The y-axis has you maintaining equilibrium between the oncoming water and the backwash of the hole. Then there is the z-axis, where you have to control the elevation of the boat as well as maintain your body at the ideal elevation for that hole. Then there is the final variable: proper head and body rotation within the boat. The hole is a variable in itself. No hole is completely stable. They pulse up and down, stronger and weaker, and the sweet spot moves left and right. Perfect. The ultimate game of skill, strategy, and chance.

Often people see kayakers cartwheeling and wonder when they are going to do something different. What people don't understand is that the person in the hole is not cartwheeling for spectators' pleasure but for his or her own pleasure. Every kayaker who goes into a hole comes out knowing that he or she could do better, get more ends, get more vertical, be more in control. This is what keeps them coming back. So beware: If you learn cartwheels, you will be a changed person, totally addicted.

Marc Lyle taught me cartwheels in 1993, two weeks before the World Championships on the Ocoee. Marc was the cartwheel king from 1993 to 1997. I was an enlightened and changed man. There is something about the challenge of cartwheeling in any hole at any time and linking as many ends as you want. Of course,

there is no one in the world who can link as many ends as he or she wants, in any hole where linking ends is possible. This means that nobody is truly bored with cartwheels yet. They are addictive, because if you can do one, you want to link more. If you do six, you want to try to do eight or ten or twenty. There are a few holes where the conditions are perfect for linking ends, and people are doing upward of forty ends before getting too tired or too dizzy to continue. The only time I decide that I have had enough of regular cartwheels for the day is after I link as many as I can physically handle. Luckily, most holes aren't perfect enough to worry about that. Most of the time, even the best boaters make mistakes that cause them to fall down or flush out. This is why Ken Whiting is as addicted to cartwheels as the kid who learned them yesterday. The carrot is always out there to chase. Of course, there are many other moves to do, but most are some derivative of cartwheels.

SETTING UP CARTWHEELS

There are several notable ways to set up cartwheels for learning, and many ways for more advanced boaters. The easiest way to start is to find a hole that is on a corner of a pourover. This kind of hole allows you to paddle in from the eddy below without the hassle of trying to set up in the meat of a hole. The next easiest way is to find a hole with a wave off to the side of it so that you can front surf into the hole from the side and already be set up to initiate. Another way is to start by spinning in a hole to get set up. A cartwheel is just a vertical spin, so spinning first and then initiating is a natural progression. The key for all methods is to get set up with the bow pointed at 12 o'clock in front of the sweet spot of the hole. For the purposes of this discussion, we are going to be cartwheeling to the left, just as we did with retendos.

Paddle position and movement. Your paddle should be doing the initiation strokes. Most people are too slow in the transition between the bow initiation and the stern initiation stroke. The result is that the boat stalls on the bow and shoots up in the air. As soon as the bow goes under the water, switch from the left blade doing the bow initiation stroke to the right blade. This switch helps keeps the boat rotating and gives you more time to control where the stern is going to land. Remember that you want the stern to land in the sweet spot at 11 to 12 o'clock. Keep the right blade in the water and look at the sweet spot. If the boat is not coming around far enough to hit the sweet spot, you need to pull quickly on the stern initiation stroke. If it is coming around too far, you need to wait before you pull, so the stern can hit at

11 to 12 o'clock. Unless you are totally vertical, the quicker and harder you pull on the stern initiation stroke (forward sweep on the right), the lower the angle of the stern. If you pull too early and hard, the boat will land in a side surf on your right side. If you are too late or too weak on your stern initiation stroke, you will land the stern at 1 o'clock or higher and "go over the top." This means that you will be upside down rolling in the hole.

Body position and movement. The most important element of body movement is that less is best. Your goal when cartwheeling is to have your body in position from the start and keep it there. If you throw your body around, you will affect many other elements of the cartwheel and you will surely flush out and fall down. Your body position is neutral and rotated to the left as much as possible. Your head should be neutral when initiating the bow and as far left as possible as soon as the bow is under the water. This keeps you

1. Setting up is everything.

2. This is the moment you finish your initiation stroke and switch to your stern stroke.

4. End of the stern stroke, with body still wound and forward.

3. Stern stroke is ready but not used unless needed before the stern hits the water.

5. Pull forward if necessary to stay in the hole and get a third end.

looking at the sweet spot for the maximum amount of time possible. For example, if you keep your head in the neutral position, you will not see the sweet spot until your bow is coming down to it. If your head and body are fully rotated to the left, you will see the sweet spot for at least twice as long.

Boat position and movement. The boat will be going end over end in the hole while on edge, like a cartwheel you would do in gym class. Specifically, your goal is to have the bow hit the sweet spot and the boat rotate around your body while your body stays in one place. You are trying to avoid having the boat fly up in the air when you initiate the bow and then crash down into the hole again for the stern. This is fun but not productive when trying to learn how to link cartwheels.

Begin by setting the boat up in front of the sweet spot. Now drop your left edge 45 to 60 degrees and use the retendo technique for initiating the bow. After the bow is under, your goal is to get the stern to land in the sweet spot at the same spot and same angle (11 to 12 o'clock) as the bow. You need to lock your hips so that you can hold the same 45 to 60 degrees of edge in the water. If you want to go more vertical, drop more edge (60 to 85 degrees). The higher the angle, the harder it is to keep your balance.

LINKING ENDS

Linking cartwheels requires that you learn how to do one cartwheel properly, then learn the techniques for putting them together. The biggest challenge in linking cartwheels is to be in position to initiate the bow after doing your first cartwheel. The third end is the hardest hurdle to get past. After that, it is simply learning how to adjust yourself in the middle of cartwheels to keep going. The most common mistake in linking ends is flushing out of the hole after two ends. This is because most holes are not very retentive and require special attention to stay in them.

Linking in Nonretentive Holes

The first key to linking in nonretentive holes (75 percent of all holes you will play in) is to adjust your initiation strokes to help you stay in the hole. It may even be necessary to add one stroke to each end you throw, without it looking like an extra stroke. The second key is to go less vertical. By keeping the boat elevation down between 45 and 60 degrees, you don't expose as much surface area of the kayak to oncoming water, but you do expose more of it to the backwash of the hole. The third key is to keep your body and strokes ahead of the boat and not let yourself get behind. Any time you try to catch up to the boat, you force yourself out of the hole. Finally, keep your body still. If you let your body drop back when the stern hits, you will wash out and not be able to hit your third end. All these keys are self-explanatory except the initiation strokes.

Paddle position and movement. Your initiation strokes must not push or pull you out of the hole. Unfortunately, most people haven't figured that one out. Sit in a chair and pretend that you are about to initiate the bow to the left. Start with your right hand up high by your head. If you did a bow initiation stroke (backsweep) from that position, which way would it push your body? It would push it backward. If you were in a hole, it would pull you out of the hole. Now start over and put your right arm as straight as possible and your left arm farther back toward the stern. If you did a strong initiation stroke now, what would it do to your body? It would push it upward, which is better than back out of the hole. Let's try the stern initiation stroke now. While sitting in a chair, put your right arm forward in the stern initiation stroke position (like a forward sweep). Keep your left hand straight out in front of you as well. If you did a strong initiation stroke (forward sweep) from this position, what would it do to your body? It would pull it forward out of the hole. This is what happens to most people. They get their second end, but when they are ready for the third end, they are not near the initiation spot anymore. Now try again with your left arm back by your left ear and your right arm fully extended. If you did a strong initiation stroke now, what would happen? You would be lifting your bow up instead of pulling your body out of the hole. This is more retentive.

There are two more steps you can take to ensure that your strokes are helping you instead of hurting you. If you pause with your stern initiation stroke until the stern hits the water and the bow begins to go up before you apply power to it, you will be able to throw the bow upstream with the stroke instead of pulling the stern downstream. Sit in a chair or lie on the ground and put yourself in the position you would be in if your stern were going under. Put your paddle in the forward sweep position and push the bow upstream. The same is true with the bow initiation stroke. If you wait until the bow is under the water before applying power (this is for the third end or more), you will be able to throw the stern upstream instead of pulling the bow downstream. Finally, you can add a stroke to each end to stay retentive. The added stroke is actually a compound stroke that looks as if it is part of the initiation stroke.

After the bow goes in the water, you have two options for retentive strokes before you initiate your stern:

1. Take a backstroke with your right blade, and convert that backstroke into your stern initiation stroke. This is essentially a short backstroke and then an immediate forward sweep. It just so happens that the paddle has to make this motion anyway to get from the bow initiation stroke into the stern initiation stroke position.
2. Do an open-faced draw to push you back into the hole and convert that into your stern initiation stroke. This method doesn't slow the rotation of the kayak as much as the first way does; however, it is not as strong.

After the stern goes in the water, you have one option for a retentive stroke before initiating the bow again: When the bow is still in the air, reach forward with the left blade and take a forward stroke until you are ready to initiate the bow. Then convert the forward stroke into the bow initiation stroke.

These techniques will make the difference between staying in the hole or washing out.

Linking Ends in Very Strong Holes
Strong holes try to throw you upstream. When you get thrown upstream, your boat hits too much of the oncoming water and it thrusts you into the foampile with more force than most people can control. Your goal with really strong holes is to hold yourself back away from the "green water" and to cartwheel in the foampile. The techniques have the opposite goal of those discussed for nonretentive holes.

Beginning with the first end:
1. Get on top of the foampile and begin your initiation stroke about 1 foot from the green water. You are trying to force the bow (or stern) through the foampile into the green water underneath.

2. Immediately after the bow goes under, switch to the stern initiation stroke and do it. Try to pull yourself downstream as you do this stroke. If you hesitate, you will get thrown upstream.

3. As soon as the stern goes under, switch to the bow initiation stroke and push hard on it, trying to hold yourself back in the foampile.

Paddle position and movement. Keep your paddle ahead of the cartwheels. This means switch and be ready for each end immediately after the previous end. Strong holes tend to have fast water and want to cartwheel you fast. You must be faster than your cartwheels, or you will fall behind and lose control. Keep the paddle vertical in the water on your initiation strokes so that you can pull yourself downstream with each stroke.

Body position and movement. Your body must stay ahead of the boat. Keep your head and body rotated to the left so that you don't get behind the boat and fall down. It is very difficult to catch up to the boat once you are behind. Keep your weight in the neutral position so that the boat doesn't bob up and down too much.

Boat position and movement. Strong holes are easier to cartwheel vertically than at a low angle. By going vertical, the boat is exposed to enough green water under the foampile to keep you from getting thrown upstream as easily. Keep the boat perfectly edged to the water and vertical.

Linking Lots of Ends

Linking many ends (anything over six) requires that you pay attention to boat placement during the cartwheels. Getting six ends or fewer can be done just by starting in the right spot of a good hole. Getting more than six requires constant attention to where you are. You must also be able to make adjustments to your elevation, speed, retentiveness, and where you are hitting your ends. Ideally, you would just use textbook-perfect cartwheel technique and not need any adjusting. Unfortunately, that rarely happens to even the best cartwheelers. You must constantly maintain your position in the hole, which adds to your list of things to do:

1. Find a hole that is retentive enough to allow you to link lots of ends.

2. Always begin every initiation with the intent of getting lots of ends. This means that you shouldn't rush to start the first end. Make sure that you are ready, are in position, and have thought it through.

3. Focus on perfect technique. In particular, keep your head and body leading the boat. Spot the hole with your eyes as much as possible to give yourself the maximum amount of time to make adjustments.

4 . Determine why you fell down or flushed out after each ride. Work on those weaknesses until they are no longer a problem. Often, letting your weight go back in the boat when the stern hits is a problem.

5. Try different rates of speed for switching from one stroke to the next. Most people switch too slowly.

6. Start by working on lower-angle cartwheels. It is better practice to link ten ends with only five being over 45 degrees than to link four vertical ends. You are working on getting quantity, not verticality. After you can link as many low-angle ends as you want, begin to elevate them until you are vertical.

7. Learn to splitwheel. Splitwheels are a way to increase the number of ends you link, because sometimes you can't keep going one way if you get out of position. If you split and go the other way, you can continue to link ends.

MOVE	Clean Cartwheel
WKF DEFINITION	Two linked ends with only one stroke, elevated 45 degrees or more. Can also be any end done with no stroke in the middle of a series of linked ends.
WKF SCORING	The same technical scoring as cartwheels, with 1 point added to your variety multiplier.

Clean cartwheels are simply one-stroke cartwheels. They are good for fun, for practice, or to get points in a rodeo. The technique for doing clean cartwheels is the same as for linking ends. The only difference is that you must be completely balanced because you don't have a paddle in the water to support you.

CLEANING THE STERN

Initiate the bow, and immediately after the bow goes under, freeze your body in the rotated position until the stern hits the water and goes through. After the stern hits, get ready to initiate the bow again. If you want to assure your friends that you are doing clean cartwheels, grab the side of the boat you are cartwheeling on. If you are cartwheeling left, grab the left side of the boat with your right hand. This helps keep your body rotated and prevents you from automatically putting your paddle in the water. This move is identical to the cartwheel. Practicing and getting your balance are all you need to succeed.

CLEANING THE BOW

Initiate the bow, then the stern, then freeze in the rotated position. It is easy to keep the paddle in your hands and wait for the bow to go under. This is also called a "washout." It is often necessary to throw your body forward to assist the bow in going under. In nonretentive holes, it is very difficult to continue linking ends after doing a clean cartwheel because you are missing a retentive stroke that will keep you in the hole.

OTHER VARIATIONS OF CARTWHEELS

Stalling. Slow down the cartwheels by hanging on the initiation stroke. You can even push backward on the initiation stroke after the end starts going under to stall the boat vertically.

Popping. Push yourself high in the air when cartwheeling, using the same technique for doing a high ender off a wave. Push on the paddle and stand up on your footbraces, then slam the stern through with a strong initiation stroke.

1. Learn by initiating at lower angle to stay more retentive, here at 1 o'clock instead of 12.

3. Keep your body wound, waiting for the stern to hit, body neutral.

2. Initiate with gusto to get lots of spin momentum on the first end.

4. Keep your weight over the boat to avoid falling on your face.

5. Wait until your bow is ready to initiate to get an official clean cartwheel before touching the water with your paddle.

6. Initiate and keep on going!

MOVE	Airwheel
WKF DEFINITION	**A cartwheel in which the boat goes high enough to bring the stern through without it supporting any of the paddler's weight.**
WKF SCORING	**A technical bonus of 4 points is given to the normal cartwheel score; 1 point is added to your variety multiplier.**

Getting airwheels requires you to pop yourself high in the air and keep the boat rotating. It is similar to a flip off a wave but is done sideways. The boat rarely does an entire flip in the air. Instead, the stern comes through before its volume is supporting the boat again. To get the boat high enough, you need to put more of it in the green water than for normal cartwheels. When the boat begins to rise back up, push as hard as you can on the bow initiation stroke to help the water lift you up. Throw your body upward to get more air. At the peak of your ascent, throw your body back to the neutral position and do the stern initiation stroke as hard as you can to try to rotate the boat through the water before you stop coming down.

MOVE	Splitwheel
WKF DEFINITION	**A cartwheel that initiates on the left and does a half twist to initiate on the right for the second end (or one that starts on the right and finishes on the left). At least one of the ends must be vertical, and the other must be at least 45 degrees. The ends must be linked.**
WKF SCORING	**Normal cartwheel scoring, with a 4-point technical bonus for the split; 1 point is added to your variety multiplier.**

One week before the 1993 World Championships on the Ocoee, I decided that it would be cool if I could do a cartwheel with a half twist. The splitwheel was born on my next ride. The move seemed easier to me than the normal cartwheel, because I could keep my paddle in the water for the whole move. A large part of why I won the Worlds that year was because I was the only one doing splitwheels. Since I wasn't linking more than two ends, the actual benefits to "splitting" weren't discovered until later.

Besides being a showy move that is more fun than a straight cartwheel, one obvious benefit is that the split allows you to change the direction you are cartwheeling without breaking your link. In rodeo, any time you have to stop what you are doing to set up another move is a waste of valuable seconds when you are not scoring any points. The split allows you to cartwheel in one direction, get a splitwheel (and all the points that go with it), and then cartwheel in the other direction, all without stopping your cartwheels. The second benefit is that if you are not in position to hit your stern during a cartwheel (as is often the case), you can split and keep going. It is a safety net during a cartwheel sequence.

For the discussion about splitting, let's assume that you are initiating the bow to the left to start.

Paddle position and movement. Use your bow initiation stroke to begin, but don't take the stroke out of the water. Once the boat is overhead and you have pirouetted 180 degrees to do the split, use the paddle to initiate the stern with a stern initiation stroke. The paddle does a push-pull motion. A push gets the bow under, then a pull gets the stern under. All these paddle strokes occur without taking the paddle out of the water.

Body position and movement. You have a choice as to how to do the splitwheel. If you want to do only a splitwheel without linking cartwheels to it, you may want to "pop" it up in the air more by standing on the footbraces before slamming the stern. If you want to link ends before and after splitting, keep your body in the neutral position for the entire move. Remember that as soon as you rotate the boat with your hips, you will begin cartwheeling to the right. This means that you need to rotate your head and torso to the right to keep ahead of the move. Lead every turn with your head and body. It is easy to let your body fall back when the stern hits the water. You need to hold yourself in the neutral position with your stomach muscles.

Boat position and movement. Start by initiating the bow as you would for a normal cartwheel. As soon as the stern is slightly upstream of the bow, pirouette the boat 180 degrees to the left (counter-clockwise) by lifting on your right knee. Drop the stern in the water at 1 o'clock. Bring the bow vertically over your head. Set the bow down at 1 o'clock to complete the move. The boat must go vertical on either the bow or the stern. When learning the move, it is possible to go low angle on both the bow and the stern to get the feel for the motion. If you rotate the boat a full 180 degrees on the bow and stern (the ends hit the water near 12 o'clock for both ends) and go low angle, that is an elevated shuvit and scores as a shuvit, not a splitwheel.

Splitting on the stern instead of the bow isn't called a splitwheel. It is changing direction during cartwheels. Athough this maneuver is good to learn, it isn't a move in itself. You have to wait until the bow is almost ready to hit the water before changing direction. Flatten out the boat and lean it the other way to initiate the opposite direction.

1. Initiate vertically on the bow.

2. Stand lightly on footbraces to slow momentum, gain air.

3. Begin dropping the other edge, rotating your body the other way and keeping your weight forward.

5. Finish your stern stroke once the boat is vertical, and switch to a forward stroke.

4. Drop lots of edge to get vertical stern.

6. Finish the forward stroke to stay in the hole.

MOVE	**Loop**
WKF DEFINITION	**A double-linked ender in which your second ender starts upside down and you ender right side up. It can be done with the back ender or front ender first.**
WKF SCORING	**4 points for each ender, plus a 6-point technical bonus; 1 point is added to your variety multiplier.**

L oops are fun moves that aren't practiced very much by most people because they usually result in being flushed out of a hole. Loops were the initial cartwheels back in the days when boats were 13 feet long. In fact, we called loops cartwheels then. Loops were usually done by getting stuck in a large hole and getting out of control. A loop is a move that involves you more intimately with the green water. The result can be eyelids turned inside out and a good nasal flushing. Nonetheless, it is very satisfying to throw a successful loop, and the underwater abuse you get can be quite addictive as well. The back and front loops are discussed separately, because the techniques for each are quite different. The beauty of loops in rodeo is the big points you get for just one. First, you get 14 technical points; then you get 1 point added to your variety multiplier. Even on an otherwise good ride, one loop can give you up to 50 percent more points for your final score. They are, of course, risky. That reminds me of a quote from Frank Scully: "Why not go out on a limb? Isn't that where the fruit is?"

FRONT LOOP

Paddle position and movement. The paddle's job is to get the boat perfectly straight and then to push you up in the air during the front ender. After you are upside down, keep your paddle still. Line the boat up for the loop by holding yourself back on the foampile until you are straight and ready to go. Then take a forward stroke to get some speed down the foampile. Convert the forward stroke into a rudder to keep the boat straight as the bow hits the water. Once you are almost vertical, convert the rudder into a backstroke to push yourself as high as possible. Keep your stroke next to the boat to prevent the backstroke from turning you to the side. Once you are airborne, do the rest with your body. Some rodeo boaters like to reach a blade into the green water

to assist the boat in flipping. You can try this technique, but it usually causes the boat to go sideways.

Body position and movement. Your body starts in the neutral position before the front ender. As soon as you approach the green water, throw your weight forward to seesaw the bow down before it hits the water. Once the bow goes down, wait until you are almost vertical, and then aggressively throw your weight back and upstream. This assists the hole in popping you up and in front of the hole. When you are almost upside down and still in the air, tuck forward aggressively to flip the boat in the air as much as possible. Keep all your motions limited to front and back motions. This way, you won't throw the boat off to one side or the other. Keep your hips locked so the boat stays flat as well.

Once you land in the water, stay tucked and still until you are upright. If you don't feel the boat being righted immediately, you will have to roll up in the hole because something went wrong. It is also possible to help the boat become upright when you are upside down. As soon as you feel the boat being endered upright, let your body go from the tucked position to the back position. This makes it easier for the water to lift the boat upright. Sometimes this backfires because you twist the boat out of position when moving your weight back.

Boat position and movement. The goal is to get a front ender that throws you forward, back into the hole, and not out of the hole. After the boat lands upside down in the hole, it must remain straight until the hole enders you back upright. The technique for keeping the boat in the hole is the same as for the wave loops discussed earlier. Find the deepest and most powerful part of the hole to do the move. Get on top of the foampile, pointed upstream. Start falling straight into the hole. Just before the bow hits the hole, try to drop the bow as vertical as you can using the seesaw technique. When the bow hits the water, use your body weight to throw the boat up and into the hole. Your goal is to have the boat do as much of a flip in the air as possible, so the stern is the first thing to hit the water. You must keep the boat flat and straight during the entire process, which is the difficult part. After you land upside down, wait for the hole to ender you back up. If you landed in the green water stern first, you will ender back up immediately. If you landed on the foampile and the backwash is strong enough, you may get pulled up to the green water and endered back up, but it isn't likely. The most common problem people have is the boat position. Body movement tends to throw the boat off to the side during the front ender.

1. Set up on top of the strong, steep part of the hole.

2. Drop in deep and hard with your body slightly back.

3. Keep your body still and paddle until the boat is vertical.

5. Begin throwing your weight back again once the boat is vertical.

4. Throw your body forward hard and avoid moving your hips. (Note how my hips are a little off!)

6. Use a forward stroke to stay in the hole.

BACK LOOP

The back loop tends not to be as dramatic but is more controllable when you do your second end. It is also more likely to be retentive. As with any back move, it is more difficult to set up because you can't see where you are going,. The feeling of being front endered from upside down is a great one. The first moment you are above the water and can see again, you are standing on your footbraces.

Paddle position and movement. The back loop provides you with more opportunities for using your paddle than the front loop. Once you are set up in the back-ender position, in front of the sweet spot, you need to slow the descent of the boat to the trough of the hole. There are two options for slowing the boat. The first is to take a few forward strokes while keeping the boat straight and slowing your descent. The other is to dig your paddle deep into the green water under the foampile. Both work, and you can decide which one you like better. The second option is good if you can control the boat with one blade easily. The forward paddling looks dramatic; it looks as though you are unsuccessfully trying to scramble out of the hole. After you hit the loop, people will know what you are doing. The most critical factor in whether you will hit your loop is being perfectly straight when you get your back ender.

The back loop has an advantage over the front loop because you can cheat under the water with your paddle. Once you are upside down and have thrown your weight forward, put the paddle blade in the forward sweep position (it doesn't matter which blade you use). Having your blade in the forward sweep position allows you to keep the bow under you as the hole enders you back upright. Whichever way you feel the boat sliding off to the side, pull or push it back under you with the paddle until you are upright. You can feel which way the boat is turning by the time you are just clearing the water with your head. This is a stroke that you have to do by feel.

Body position and movement. Just before the boat hits the green water, throw your weight back to seesaw the stern down. Stay in the back position after the back ender until you feel the boat endering upright again. When you feel the boat being endered back up, bring your weight forward to help the water upright you. This motion keeps your body in the water, where it is weightless, for as long as possible. Limit body motions to either front or back movements to keep the boat from twisting off to the side.

Boat position and movement. The boat position and movement for a back loop is identical to that for a front loop. Get on top of the foampile, begin falling into the trough of the hole, seesaw the boat vertical, and keep it straight. Getting to the top of the foampile is more difficult than with the front loop. One technique is to do a 180-degree spin on the corner and then fall back into the hole. The other is to do a bow retendo; the result will face you downstream and ready to do a back loop. With less retentive and steeper holes, it helps to slow the boat down before it hits the green water. In doing so, you don't expose as much of the stern to the oncoming water and you are less likely to flush out. Throwing your weight up and back into the hole is much more difficult than with the front loop. Speed in a back loop will not help you stick it.

1. Drop into the sweet spot holding the boat straight with one blade.

3. Keep your hips still and enjoy the backender.

2. Start throwing your weight back once the stern hits.

4. Keep your weight back, hips still, and bring either blade to the bow draw position.

5. Hold steady, waiting for the bow to catch.

7. Keep your weight forward until the boat is vertical, then return to neutral position to sit the boat down. Congratulations on your loop!

6. Feeling the bow catch, throw your body back to the forward position, keeping the bow straight with a bow draw.

MOVE	Blast
WKF DEFINITION	Front or back surfing the green water in front of a hole. This can be done vertically for pourovers or horizontally for flat holes.
WKF SCORING	The same as for front and back surfing flat holes or wave-holes. For pourovers, the score is 2 points for semivertical and 4 points for vertical; .5 is added to your variety multiplier.

FRONT BLASTING

Blasting (front or back surfing) holes is one of the easiest and fastest ways to get from one side of the hole to the other. You can blast any hole, but wave-holes are the easiest. The backwash of the hole naturally pushes you in front of it. With a planing boat, you can easily go from a side surf to a blast. Every boat blasts differently. Some blast better backward than forward, and vice versa. Most of the rodeo boats blast easily.

There are two primary ways to get into a blast. The first is to start next to the wave-hole and surf in front of the foampile from the side. The other is to ride down the foampile and lean back (for a front blast) as you drop into the trough of the wave-hole into the blast position. A typical blast goes like this: You are side surfing a wave-hole and want to blast out the side of it onto the green wave. You do a strong sweep to turn the boat upstream into a blast. You will feel the foampile on your back, and the boat will bounce a little. Once you are in control, lean a little to the left to go left and pull forward on your left blade against the foampile to accelerate the boat to the side of the hole. Once clear of the hole, rudder the boat straight and surf on the wave next to the hole.

Paddle position and movement. You have two options for paddle position when blasting: the rudder position or the forward sweep–stern draw position. The rudder position does not as work as well because it pushes you into the foampile and it doesn't propel you quickly. The stern draw position gives you more speed and holds you in front of the foampile more effectively. Most wave-holes allow you to start in a side-surf position and do a strong sweep to put you in blast position. The key for controlling the blast with your sweep-stern draws is to keep the paddle in the water.

Body position and movement. Keep your body neutral whenever possible. The only time you really need to lean way back or forward is when you are dropping into a blast from the top of the foampile. Most boats have enough rocker to blast without worrying about your ends pearling. When you use heavy leans, you don't have maximum boat control, and the boat bounces around more.

Boat position and movement. When blasting, there is a lot of water speed under the boat. Therefore, any boat leans tend to have a major effect on boat position. Generally, if you are in either a forward or back blast position and you lean the boat one way, it will immediately spin in the direction of your lean. If you continue to lean the boat, you will spin into the side-surf position, unless you overpower the spin with your paddle. Thus, when

blasting, edge control is important. If you are not in control of your edges (leans), you can lose control easily. You can cut back and forth when blasting (the same as you would when surfing), as long as you keep the boat nearly flat.

BACK BLASTING

Everything is the same for back blasting, except for paddle position and movement. Control your blast with backsweeps placed in the foampile in front of you. Pay special attention to boat leans, because it is easy to lose your angle and end up side surfing. Leaning forward to reach the foampile ensures that the stern won't catch the green water.

BLASTING POUROVERS

Pourovers are a completely different type of blast than wave-holes. When blasting a pourover, you are vertical or nearly vertical. Getting into a blast and holding a blast in a pourover are much more difficult than a wave-hole blast. The ideal pourovers for blasting are about 2 feet high, vertical, with 4 to 12 inches of water going over them. The backwash should be strong all the way up to the green water. There should be an eddy behind the pourover for you to start in. It is possible to get into a blast from above or below the pourover. Here, I discuss entering the pourover from below. The technique begins with getting into the eddy behind the pourover. Start on one side of the eddy and about 5 feet below the pourover. Aim your boat at the middle of the pourover (about a 30-degree angle). Get some speed toward the pourover, and when the boat is about to hit the green water, lean on your downstream edge and take a big forward sweep–stern initiation stroke. Keep pulling on that sweep until the boat is pointed straight upstream. Your butt will be on the green water, and your boat will be nearly vertical. At this point, you will fall down to the side, the stern will float up, or you will pull yourself the final bit up into a blast. Immediately after the boat is on top of the green water, lean back and take another forward stroke (or two) until you feel the boat rise up vertically. You are now in the seam between the backwash and the green water. This is a blast.

Paddle position and movement. Once you have done the sweep initiation stroke to get the bow up and on top of the green water, you have two options for controlling the blast. The first is to do forward sweeps every time your boat starts to fall one way or another to keep it straight. The other is to use a rudder stroke to hold it straight. The forward sweeps won't make you travel one way or another in the hole. The rudder pushes your boat away from the stroke until you move out of the hole. (For example, if you have a rudder in the water on the left, your boat will travel to the right until you are out of the hole.) If you rudder too hard, you will begin to fall the other way and have to rudder on the other side. The challenge of a blast is getting vertical and holding yourself there.

Body position and movement. Your body should start in the neutral position. Throw your body back as you do your big sweep-initiation stroke to get onto the green water. Once you are totally vertical, you can go back to neutral or just keep your back on top of the backwash to help you balance.

Boat position and movement. The boat has to start at an angle to the hole. When you sweep to put the boat up on top of the green water, the boat will then be straight. Once on top of the green water, you need to get the boat totally vertical. Do this by pulling it all the way into the seam between the green water and the backwash. Once it is vertical, your goal is to keep it vertical. When you are ready to come down from the blast, you can let the bow fall one way or the other and blast out the side of the hole before falling down.

BOW BLASTING

Blasting with the bow under the water and the stern in the air is a fun trick. It requires more skill than the stern blast to get vertical initially. After you are vertical, it is just as easy. There are two ways to get vertical for a bow blast: from below the hole or from above. I'll save the one from above for the chapter on eddyline moves. Getting the bow down in a pourover into a blast position requires an effective bow initiation stroke. The move begins by starting at an angle to and below the pourover. Develop speed to do your bow initiation stroke as you paddle at a sharp angle to the pourover. Initiate the bow in the green water of the pourover at about 9:30 to 10 o'clock. Just barely put the bow into the green water (so you don't hit the rock). Initiate the bow until you are vertical, and then twist the boat to sit flat against the green water. Keep your weight in the neutral position until the boat is totally vertical and blasting. Use backsweeps on either side to keep the boat vertical. Stand on your footbraces if you want to have a look around. This is a cool move.

Paddle position and movement. Use the bow initiation stroke to get vertical. Keep your blade from the bow initiation stroke in the water. Doing this will control the boat until you are vertical and balanced. Once you are vertical and blasting, use reverse sweeps (slap strokes on top of the backwash) to keep yourself vertical.

Body position and movement. Your body's job is to put everything into the bow initiation stroke. This means that you have to throw your body forward when you first initiate the bow to ensure that you go vertical. After that, stay neutral until you are blasting and balanced. You can stand on your footbraces any time you wish.

Boat position and movement. The boat must start at a sharp angle to the pourover and a few feet below it. Initiate the bow in the seam between the green water and the backwash at 9:30 to 10 o'clock. Don't expose too much of the bow to the green water, or you will slam the rock that makes the pourover. Bring the boat vertical using the initiation stroke and help from the green water. Once you are vertical, rotate the boat to sit flat against the green water. You are now blasting. Keep it vertical.

BLASTING CARTWHEELS

After becoming proficient in both bow and stern blasts in a pourover, you are ready to do blasting cartwheels, or cartwheels done while you are blasting. Unlike with normal cartwheels, your boat will be cartwheeling across the river instead of up and down it. Your body will be facing downstream, and the boat will cartwheel parallel to the seam line of the pourover. This move takes solid boat control and power, unless your boat is really low volume.

Paddle position and movement. Your paddle's job is to do strong initiation strokes to pull the ends through. If you are weak on initiation strokes, you will be side surfing the pourover. You must also keep yourself vertical in the blast position in between ends. Use the blasting techniques listed in the previous section for that.

Body position and movement. Your body should move only forward or backward to help you initiate the ends. If you are going from a bow blast to a stern blast, lean back as you slam the stern, and vice versa.

Boat position and movement. It is easier to start in the bow blast position, because it is easier to slam the stern than the bow. (If you can't get into the bow blast position, you probably can't do blasting cartwheels either.) Once in the bow blast position, let the stern begin to fall into the seam of the pourover. Just before it hits the water, initiate the stern in the seam and bring the stern completely under you. Keep the boat totally vertical so that you are slamming partially into the green water instead of only through the backwash. Control the stern blast as discussed earlier. To link ends, all you have to do is let the bow drop into the seam between the backwash and the green water. Initiate the bow just before it hits the water. Keep the bow in the green water as much as possible so the backwash doesn't reject it.

MOVE	Counter Clock Wheel
WKF DEFINITION	Getting vertical in a hole by rotating the boat downstream instead of upstream. The boat is working against the current.
WKF SCORING	A technical score of 4 points is given only if the boat goes totally vertical; .75 is added to your variety multiplier.

The counter clock wheel (CCW) is is difficult to do in most holes but is very cool when it is done well. It usually looks like the boater is really winding up before throwing the first end. The CCW is done on the backwash of a hole. The bow is thrown in the air with either a forward sweep or a squirt stroke, and then slammed down into regular cartwheels. The best holes for this move are ones with a large retentive backwash that is flat and easy to balance on. The move is easiest when you can get into equilibrium. If the boat is on end in the backwash and the amount of boat in the green water and the backwash is the same, you will be in equilibrium. A squirt boater on the Ottawa in a C-1 invented the move. Because of the ideal conditions it requires, not many people do this move. Keep your eyes open for opportunities to try it. It is a unique feeling winding up against the current and then slamming the bow back down.

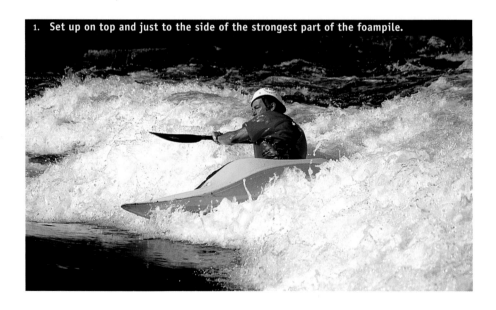

1. Set up on top and just to the side of the strongest part of the foampile.

2. Do a strong squirt stroke, slicing the edge exactly upstream. Expect to go deep.

3. Switch from the squirt stroke to a stern initiation stroke to slam the bow back down from where it came.

4. Coming back down, slightly out of control.

5. Finishing in the hole.

MOVE	**Mystery Move**
WKF DEFINITION	**Submerging the entire boat and body using the green water of a hole.**
WKF SCORING	**Technical score of 4 points; .75 is added to your variety multiplier.**

The mystery move has long been the domain of squirt boaters. Since rodeo boats have become lower volume and flatter, mystery moves have become possible and even fairly easy. The objective of a mystery move is simply downtime. The deeper you go and the longer you stay down, the better the mystery move. In pourovers, it is possible to add mystery moves to your ride without flushing out of the hole. Controlled resurfacing back into the hole is the second major objective. In most pourovers, the side with the most water is best for mystery moves. This is usually where the hole is the most powerful.

Paddle position and movement. Start by paddling into the hole fast. As soon as the bow goes down, do a reverse sweep on the downstream side to push the rest of the boat into the hole sideways. Keep your downstream paddle in the water. Keep pressure on the paddle toward the pourover with your reverse sweep. This pressure helps keep you in the downwater.

Body position and movement. Start with your body in the neutral position. Lean forward when the bow hits. When you sweep the stern into the hole, bring your body back to neutral. If you lean back, the bow will come up immediately. Keep your weight over the boat. Don't lean downstream or upstream. You won't power flip if you keep your weight over the boat

and let the bow go down before exposing your entire side to the green water.

Boat position and movement. Start with the boat at a 45-degree angle to the pourover. Get as much speed as possible toward the hole. Drive the bow into the hole at a 45-degree angle with a flat boat. As soon as the bow starts going down, place the entire boat into the hole by reverse sweeping the stern into the hole. The boat should be leaning slightly downstream. The exact angle of lean should be less than that of the green water, so the green water can pile up onto the deck. When you sweep the stern into the hole, try to keep the boat parallel to the hole so that the bow and stern are still being forced down. Most people sweep the stern in too hard and the bow rises immediately.

CHAPTER NINE

Rock Moves

Using rocks to do moves has been increasing at an incredible rate. The creation of plastic boats that bow squirt has opened up many new possibilities for rock moves. The combination of wavewheels, cartwheels, mystery moves, and rock moves makes river running more interesting than ever before.

MOVE	**Rock Spin**
WKF DEFINITION	**A 360-degree or greater spin on top of a rock with the kayak completely out of the water.**
WKF SCORING	**Scored for freestyle through a rapid competition. Scores 6 points for a complete 360-degree spin and an additional 2 points for each additional 180 degrees after the 360; .75 is added to your variety multiplier.**

Rock spins are impressive if they are done well on a rock that is high out of the water. The ability to gauge a rock for height and slipperiness and the speed of the water takes practice. Fortunately, most river runs have an abundance of rocks to practice on. Rock spins become addictive, and it becomes impossible to pass up an opportunity to do one.

Deciding which rocks are good and which ones aren't requires a little experience. On some rivers, the rocks are slippery and smooth, allowing you to get up high on them and spin easily. Some rocks are grabby and difficult to get on top of (plus they tear up your boat). The factors you must look for when picking rocks are:
- The height of the rock
- The platform on top of the rock (large and flat or very small and pointed)
- The amount of current that is carrying you to the rock
- The texture of the rock (slippery or grabby)
- What's behind the rock

Ideally, the rock is 1 to 2 feet out of the water, slippery, and flat, with quick current leading to it. This type of rock is the easiest to get on top of and to stay on while spinning. Look to make sure there isn't another rock immediately behind the one you are spinning on, because you wouldn't want to fall on it with your ribs or shoulders.

Paddle position and movement. Start with fast forward strokes to get the boat moving toward the rock at the correct speed. When you are about to hit the rock, take a strong forward sweep. Your goal with the forward sweep is to get on top of the rock and to start the boat spinning in the direction you want. Take your sweep on the side that will rotate your boat the way you want to spin. This forward sweep should be the last stroke you take to get on the rock. Immediately switch to a reverse sweep on the other side to get the boat spinning quickly. If you wait too long to take the reverse sweep, you may not reach the water. Once you have taken the reverse sweep, you should be spinning. Ideally, you won't need any more strokes to complete your spin. However, as often as not, the boat will catch on something, and you will need one more stroke to complete the spin. Your next stroke may be against the rock because you can't reach the water. After your reverse sweep, look for something to sweep against to continue the spin. It doesn't matter whether it is a forward or reverse sweep. Normally, you will slide off the rock effortlessly. However, if you get stuck, you will have to pull yourself off.

Body position and movement. Start with your body in neutral position until you are sweeping onto the rock. Lean back on your sweep to help get the bow up onto the rock. As soon as your butt is on the crest of the rock, lean forward hard to seesaw the boat flat on top of the rock. Rotate your head and body in the direction you want to spin at the same time you are throwing your weight forward. Once you are on top of the rock, keep your body rotated but go back to the neutral position. A slick way to do a 360-degree rock spin is to do your initial reverse sweep and then put your hand on top of your head while you spin like a top. After you do exactly a 360-degree spin, lean way forward; that will stop you from rotating and help you slide off the rock. It looks more controlled, instead of looking like you tried to get more than you did.

Boat position and movement. Start directly upstream of the rock and begin to paddle toward it. Gauge your speed so that the boat will slide on top of the rock and stall there. If you don't have enough speed, the boat will not make it to the top. Too much speed will send you over the top before you have a chance to spin. Just as you are about to hit the rock head-on, lift the bow with a forward sweep to get the bow on top of the rock. Your speed will carry you the rest of the way. As soon as you are almost out of the water, begin your spin in the direction you choose. Get the boat spinning as fast as possible before you get completely on top of the rock. If you wait until you are on top, you may not reach the water, and you may slide off before completing your spin. The direction you spin is determined by your approach to the rock. If you are coming to the rock from a slightly left approach, you will likely need to spin to the right. The water hitting your stern as you climb the rock will try to spin you right, so why fight it? After you have done your spin, drop off the rock flat so that you are balanced and the boat is under you. Try to avoid dropping off the rock leaning to the side and bracing. You never know when you will land on another rock with your body. It is also possible to drop off the back of the rock vertically into a splat. Use the same technique, but lean to seesaw the boat vertically as you are coming off the rock.

1. Begin a back sweep just as your stern clears the water.

2. Keep your weight neutral to allow the boat to spin in the middle.

3. Forward sweep if necessary to keep the boat spinning.

4. Try to keep your body leading the spin.

5. Get all you can get as you are sliding off, and go for another spin.

6. Lean toward the water to help the boat slide off the rock at the chosen time.

7. Go on your way.

MOVE	Rock Splat
WKF DEFINITION	Getting your boat vertical against a rock, either bow or stern.
WKF SCORING	4 technical points for the vertical end; .5 is added to your variety multiplier.

Rock splats are another fun way to get vertical and enjoy rocks. People have been doing rock splats even before boats could be squirted. Dancers, Crossfires, and other huge pre-rodeo boats were being splatted. Now with squirtable bows and sterns, rock splats have become very easy moves and are almost as common as the cartwheel. A word of warning, though: Always know the rock or wall you are splatting. Splatting undercut walls or rocks can ruin your day. If you are in doubt, don't splat it. After you have lots of experience reading water and you can read rocks and walls well, you can splat new places. Remember, it takes only one major mistake to end your kayaking career. Another hazard to look for is nasty rocks behind your splat rock. Often, you will wash off a rock, upside down. A barely submerged rock below can wreak havoc with your face, shoulders, and ribs.

BOW SPLATS

The most common splatting technique is with the bow in the air. Let's learn how to splat a big, flat wall with a nice fold in front of it. If you can splat walls, you can splat any rock if you have a good squirt stroke or stern initiation stroke. If you can already stern splat, go to the next section on splatwheels.

Paddle position and movement. You can use either a squirt stroke on the downstream side or a stern initiation stroke on the upstream side of the boat to get the bow up on the rock. If you can't squirt very well, use the stern initiation stroke until you get better at squirting. Once you are vertical on the rock, use forward sweeps on either side to keep the boat vertical.

Body position and movement. Start with your body in the neutral position.

Lean back, but keep your weight over the boat until you get the boat vertical. Once vertical, it is easiest to balance with your back resting on the water.

Boat position and movement. The easiest way to start a bow splat is to have the boat pointed downstream and right on the seam between the current and the pillow off the rock. The bow should be about 2 to 3 feet from the rock, and your body should be on the seam. Lean the boat upstream about 30 degrees and do a big stern initiation stroke. The bow will lift up and hit the rock. Keep your forward sweep (stern initiation stroke) in the water and pull the boat all the way vertical against the rock. Try to keep the boat vertical until you want to come down. Often there is current running along the rock you are splatting and you can slide along the rock to the end of it.

STERN SPLATS

Stern splats can be done with a boat with a squirtable bow. There are two main methods of stern splatting (stern against the wall). The first is similar to the bow splat, and the second requires you to get the bow down and the boat vertical in flatwater. Let's start with the standard splat technique.

Paddle position and movement. After you back into the rock and drop your upstream edge, do a strong reverse sweep to get the bow under the water and pointed directly into the oncoming water. Keep that backstroke in the water and apply as much pressure against the oncoming water as you can until the boat is vertical. Once you are vertical, keep yourself vertical by using bracing backstrokes on either side.

Body position and movement. Start in the neutral position and then lean hard forward as you try to get the bow down. Once you are vertical, you can go back to the neutral position.

Boat position and movement. Back into the rock you want to splat. It must have current coming into the fold toward the rock. Let the stern hit the rock, and let the boat get a little sideways (about 10 to 30 degrees). Now drop your upstream edge about 20 to 30 degrees and initiate the bow under the water. The oncoming current will ender you up against the rock or wall. If the current isn't strong enough to take you up, either wait for a surge that is strong enough or find another rock.

FLYING STERN SPLATS

If you can get the boat vertical on the bow in flatwater, you can do flying stern splats. To do a flying stern splat, you must be going at least as fast as the current toward or parallel to a rock you wish to splat and initiate the bow in the fold before you hit the rock. You will slam the rock or slide along it in the stern splat position (stern in the air). The flying stern splat is the easiest way to start splatwheels on walls.

Paddle position and movement. This is just a bow initiation against a rock.

Body position and movement. Same as a bow initiation in a hole or flatwater.

Boat position and movement. You have two options (and anywhere in between) to set up a flying stern splat. The first is to splat walls or rocks on the side that parallels the current. If you are splatting the side of a rock, you can set it up best by coming straight downstream and initiating the bow right next to the rock. You will slide along the rock. If you are splatting the upstream side of a rock, come straight down on it. Initiate the bow just before you hit the rock. You will go vertical and be able to drop against the rock.

To splat the side of a rock:
1. Paddle fast enough to initiate the bow right next to the rock.
2. Initiate the bow right next to the rock in the fold between the slow water and the current.
3. Sit the boat against the rock with the hull sliding along it.

To splat the front of a rock:
1. Paddle fast enough toward the rock to initiate the bow.
2. Initiate the bow right next to the rock at the last possible moment before you hit it.
3. Twist the boat to hit the rock hull-first after you get vertical (90-degree pirouette).

MOVE	Splatwheel
WKF DEFINITION	Cartwheels done against a rock or wall; must be elevated 45 degrees or higher. They can be done with the boat partially supported by a rock or totally supported in the water.
WKF SCORING	2 technical points for each end 45 to 70 degrees in elevation, 4 technical points for each end 71 to 90 degrees in elevation; .75 is added to your variety multiplier for both right and left splatwheels.

Splatwheels were a move initially done by squirt boaters and adopted by rodeo boaters thanks to new boat designs that make splatwheels possible. They are done in the freestyle through a rapid event in rodeos and on rivers everywhere. There are two kinds of splatwheels: those done by paddling partially up on a rock and then splatwheeling, and those done against a wall and rocks where you are totally supported by the water. Splatwheels supported by the water are essentially flatwater cartwheels.

SPLATWHEELS IN THE WATER

The easiest way to do splatwheels along walls or against rocks is to first initiate the bow for a stern splat and then slam the stern to complete a cartwheel. It is easiest to cartwheel with the current instead of against it. When you pull your ends through, they go with the current. You can get a third end if you stay balanced and fairly vertical after your second end. Getting the bow down the second time is easier in a splat than in flatwater because the current helps you.

SPLATWHEELS ON A ROCK

Doing splatwheels partially supported by a rock is identical to doing a rock spin, except you don't go as high up on the rock.

Paddle position and movement. Your last stroke as you forward sweep the boat onto the rock should begin to spin the boat. Immediately switch to a reverse sweep to finish spinning the boat the first 180 degrees. (At this point, the bow will be hitting the water.) Keep your reverse sweep in the water and convert it into a bow initiation stroke. Once you have pulled the bow through, switch to a stern initiation stroke (see flatwater cartwheels).

Body position and movement. As you get the boat partially on the rock, you should still be in the neutral or back position (if you needed to go back to get the bow up on the rock). Rotate your head and body in the direction you want to spin. Throw your weight forward as you begin your spin. When you throw your weight forward, you cause the bow to drop more vertically after the first 180-degree spin and hit the water. This is the beginning of the cartwheel. Go back to a neutral position to slam the stern, and then forward to initiate the bow again.

Boat position and movement. Start above the rock you want to splatwheel. Generate enough speed to get most of the boat out of the water. As soon as your butt hits the rock, begin an aggressive spin (it is easier to spin to the left if you are slightly on the right side of the rock, and vice versa). The bow will hit the water, but it will slice through easily if you are partially on the rock. You may be able to slam the stern before you completely slide back into the water. If you can do this, the stern will slice easily through the water. You can again initiate your bow using a strong bow initiation stroke.

1. Initiate the bow next to the wall.

2. Let the stern hit the wall before slamming it.

3. Initiate the stern.

4. Perched on a wall for close inspection of the local geology.

CHAPTER TEN

Eddyline Moves

MOVE	**Eddyline Cartwheel**
WKF DEFINITION	**Cartwheels done on an eddyline.**
WKF SCORING	**2 technical points for each end at 45 to 70 degrees of elevation and 4 points for each end at 71 to 110 degrees of elevation; .75 is added to your variety multiplier.**

Eddyline cartwheels were the predecessor to flatwater cartwheels for rodeo boats. Getting the first bow down is much easier on an eddyline than in flatwater. Whether it is any easier on an eddyline after the first end is questionable, because the eddyline can make balancing more difficult. The cool thing about eddyline cartwheels is that you can do them on the way into an eddy as well as on the way out. It certainly makes catching eddies more interesting.

Paddle position and movement. Same as the initiation stroke in flatwater.

Body position and movement. Same as the inittiation stroke in flatwater.

Boat position and movement. Starting in an eddy, get some speed toward the eddyline almost parallel to it. As soon as the bow crosses the eddyline, do a strong bow initiation stroke on the current side of the eddyline. The goal is to do the initiation stroke just as your body is on the eddyline. Your boat should be as parallel to the eddyline as possible. If you try to initiate the bow and it doesn't go under but gets swept downstream, you are angled into the current too much. If you can't get the bow down very far in flatwater with the bow initiation stroke, you will have difficulty getting cartwheels. Look for very sharp eddylines with no boils;

boils make the move more difficult. Once the boat is vertical, slam the stern and stay parallel to the eddyline if possible. Continue cartwheeling as much as you want using the flatwater cartwheel technique described in the next chapter.

Alternatively, come down to the eddy nearly parallel to the eddyline. Aim for the sharpest part of the eddyline. As soon as the bow crosses the eddyline, do the initiation stroke on the eddy side of the boat. Eddyline cartwheels going into an eddy are physically easier (take less strength) because you have much more speed than when starting in the eddy. Even though the bow hits the same current as when you are doing a cartwheel on the way out, it is easier going in because your momentum carries you into the eddy and helps subsidize your initiation stroke with its own energy. It is possible to initiate in the opposite direction suggested for both going in and coming out of an eddy. It is just a little more difficult and more like doing flatwater cartwheels. It is your choice.

1. Initiate on the eddyline.

3. Slam the stern as it hits the water.

2. Keep your edge in line with the eddyline.

4. Keep it going.

MOVE	Plowing Ender
WKF DEFINITION	**See Enders.**
WKF SCORING	**See Enders.**

Plowing enders are a neat way to get vertical. Create your own wave by paddling fast, then slow down and begin endering on your own wave. You can finish off the ender by crossing the eddyline with the bow under the water. The fast current will ender you up. Certain rodeo boats allow you to do this in flatwater if you have good technique and enough body weight (or a small enough boat). Start by paddling forward with lots of speed to create a wake, then slow down dramatically while leaning forward. The bow will begin to submerge. As soon as the bow goes under the water, begin to paddle hard. Keep the boat flat and straight until you ender up vertically. On an eddyline, the technique is identical. After the bow submerges, the current will help ender you up. Timing is the key to the success of the plowing ender. Try to get the bow under before you cross the eddyline. The current will catch the bow as soon as it crosses. If you try to get the bow under after you cross the eddyline, the bow will plane up and not go under. Once you are vertical, you can do pirouettes or cartwheels.

1. The bow is under before reaching the eddyline.

2. The current takes care of the rest.

3. Standing on the footbraces prolongs your air time.

MOVE	Nugget
WKF DEFINITION	A 360-degree bow pirouette into a 360-degree stern pirouette on an eddyline.
WKF SCORING	Scored as separate parts (front ender, pirouette, back ender, and pirouette).

A nugget is done off a plowing ender on an eddyline.

Paddle position and movement. You can use either a cross-bow stroke to pirouette the bow or a normal pirouette stroke. Use a stern initiation stroke to slam the stern, coverting that stroke into a pirouette stroke on the stern.

Body position and movement. Stand on the footbraces on the bow pirouette and fall back to neutral for the stern pirouette.

Boat position and movement. Get vertical off a plowing ender, then pirouette (see pirouette and plowing ender descriptions). After the pirouette, slam the stern and pirouette on the stern.

1. Start with a plowing ender. Shane Benedict taught me this one.

2. Get vertical on the eddyline.

3. Throw the 360-degree pirouette on one stroke.

4. Slam the stern and begin pirouetting on your next stroke.

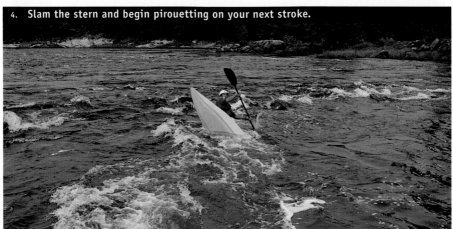

5. Finish the nugget with a full 360 pirouette on your second stroke overall.

MOVE	Squirt
WKF DEFINITION	Slicing the bow or stern under the water to get the boat vertical in a corkscrew motion.
WKF SCORING	Scored as an elevated or vertical end, with the pirouette added to the score; .5 is added to your variety multiplier.

Squirting the stern of a boat has been around for a long time. Even slalom boats squirt. The first addition to rodeo boats when they came out was a squirtable stern (1992). The squirt is still a challenging move, even though it's not new. It requires you to break a very basic rule: Always lean downstream.

Paddle position and movement. As soon as you cross the eddyline, put your downstream blade in the water in the reverse sweep position. This position is as far to the stern as you can reach. When you drop your upstream edge, give your reverse sweep as much power as you have to get the stern down. After this stroke, you are both vertical and balanced. You may want to pirouette. Do not take a stroke on the other side. Take another reverse sweep on the same side to rotate the boat more and get it higher. If you take a stroke on the other side of the boat, you are likely leaning on your stroke and using the stroke to keep your balance. You can't get good at squirting until you eliminate this stroke.

Body position and movement. Keep your body weight over the boat. Do not lean away from the boat. If you need a forward sweep to keep your balance after you do the reverse sweep, you are not staying over the boat. You should be able to do the squirt and then put the paddle in

the air and stay balanced. Start with your body in the neutral position. Drop your weight back when you begin the squirt. You can stay back or go back to neutral when the stern is under the water.

Boat position and movement. The easiest place to squirt is on a crisp eddyline. Your objective is to use the current just past the eddyline to push the stern under the water. You must help the current do this by slicing the stern under the water in the beginning. The steps are:

1. Cross the eddyline perpendicular to it. Most people are pointed upstream when they cross the eddyline. This is much more difficult than being perpendicular or even pointed slightly downstream.

2. As soon as your body is on the eddyline, drop your upstream edge 30 degrees and do your backsweep.

3. When the boat is pointed straight downstream, flatten it out (eliminate the edge being dropped) and let the current ender you the rest of the way up.

1. Beginning a reverse sweep after the bow is slightly downstream makes this move much easier.

3. Flatten out the edge at 180 degrees, keeping your weight over the boat.

2. Stay on the reverse sweep until your bow is as high as you want it.

CHAPTER ELEVEN

Flatwater Moves

Why would whitewater rodeo boaters want to do moves in flatwater? Because often there is flatwater between rapids or in eddyies, and rodeo boaters don't like to sit still. They do tricks in flatwater to stay entertained. There are really only three moves you can do in flatwater that are vertical: cartwheels (including split-wheels), pirouettes, and squirts.

MOVE	**Flatwater Cartwheel**
WKF DEFINITION	**Cartwheels done without the assistance of moving water.**
WKF SCORING	**Same as cartwheels in a hole.**

Flatwater cartwheels require skill even if you are paddling a boat that is the right size for you. They are easier in a boat that is small for you. Practice doing them until you can link four or more ends. This is a good way to improve your balance in a hole for cartwheels. Your ability to do flatwater cartwheels depends on your initiation strokes, your balance, and the type of boat you paddle. If your boat is too big, you won't be able to flatwater cartwheel. If your ability to do initiation strokes aren't very good, you won't be flatwater cartwheeling either. Assuming that you have a boat that will work for you, let's proceed.

Paddle position and movement. Your initial paddle stroke is called a double-pump initiation stroke. This is just a fancy way of saying that you lift the bow up before slamming it down. This motion generates some rotational speed before the bow hits the water. The double-pump is a bow initiation stroke (with the boat on edge about 60 degrees) to get the bow up in the air a foot or so, and then an aggressive switch to the bow initiation stroke (with the boat on edge about 80 degrees). If you are learning how to get your first end underwater, you need to practice the double-pump. After you do the double-pump, the bow should be under the water. The key to getting the boat totally vertical is what you do with your paddle at the end of the bow initiation stroke. Assuming that you are getting the bow under and the boat up at least 45 degrees, you only need to pull the bow under your body at this point. Most people try to lift the stern up, but this doesn't get the bow under you. Think of the last part of the bow initiation stroke for flatwater cartwheels as "closing the scissors." Pull the bow under you by pushing the paddle blade over the top of the deck. It looks like you are closing a pair of scissors. To put your paddle in this position, keep your top hand (non-power hand) up high so the paddle is vertical in the water. After you have the boat completely vertical on the bow, switch to a stern initiation stroke. The stern initiation stroke is a powerful forward sweep. The sooner you pull on the stern initiation stroke (after you are done with the bow stroke), the more success you will have in pulling the stern all the way through. You can stall out on the bow for fun, but it doesn't make it easier.

Body position and movement. Keep your body neutral. Go forward to help the bow go down, if necessary. Don't stand on your footbraces when on the bow if you want to link ends. This will bounce you up in the air. Don't fall back when the stern hits the water. The bow will rise up in the air and you won't be able to get it down for a third end. Keep your body rotated in the direction you are cartwheeling. This helps maintain your rotational speed and increases the number of ends you can hit.

Boat position and movement. Start with lots of forward speed. When you first initiate the bow, your speed against the water will help get the bow under you. After you are moving forward, do a double-pump bow initiation stroke to get the bow down (see paddle position and movement). You should drop your edge between 75 and 85 degrees (almost vertical). Keep your hips locked. When you do the initiation stroke, don't let the boat overrotate and tip over. You will stay balanced as long as you don't initiate totally vertical. After the bow is down, initiate the stern while maintaining the same edge angle. If you let your hips relax, the boat will get out of control, causing you to slam the stern too flat or too vertical. As soon as the boat is vertical on the stern, prepare to initiate the bow again. Getting the third end is the hardest. You must be balanced and have the proper

1. Bring the bow up with 45 degrees of edge, ready to slam.

amount of edge dropped to get the bow under again. If you are totally vertical on the stern, you are unlikely to get a third end. It is much easier to be elevated at 75 to 80 degrees than at 90 degrees. Keep as much boat rotational speed as possible during your cartwheels. One way to maintain rotational speed is to keep the boat from bouncing up or down when you cartwheel. If you bounce up on the bow, you will have to slam the stern harder and will likely lose your balance as well as speed. The ideal flatwater cartwheels are smooth, done at constant speed, without bouncing up and down, while maintaining elevation at 80 degrees.

2. Slam the bow down at close to 90 degrees. Notice the shoulders leading the body.

3. Continue on the initiation stroke until the boat is vertical. Keep your weight forward.

4. Switch from bow to stern stroke. Try to stay off the footbraces.

5. Time to slam the stern. Dropping the stern in with 90 degrees of edge is easiest.

6. Keep your shoulders from getting too far behind. A nearly vertical boat is easiest to balance.

7. With shoulders leading again, your paddle is ready for the next bow stroke with time to spare.

MOVE	Flatwater Splitwheel

The technique is identical to flatwater cartwheels with a split. See the description of splitwheels for how to split.

MOVE	Flatwater Pirouette

Initiate the bow in flatwater using the flatwater cartwheel technique, then pirouette using either a cross-bow pirouette stroke or a normal pirouette (see the descriptions of enders and pirouettes).

1. Get vertical with the bow initiation.

2. Begin pushing your paddle in front of the boat.

3. Throw your head and shoulders in the direction you want to pirouette.

4. Keep your balance after the stroke is finished by keeping your weight over the boat.

5. Another pirouette stroke.

6. Use a forward sweep to keep it going.

7. Falling on my face.

PART III

YOUR BODY: PHYSICAL TRAINING FOR PLAYBOATING AND RODEO

The only vehicle for getting you through life is your body. You can't abuse it and then trade it in for a new one when it doesn't work anymore. Is your body like a clunker car parked on the curb that gets you from birth to death any old way? Or is your body like a fine, well-oiled machine ready for Le Mans? In playboating, some people can keep going all day long, and others will get tired in the first half of the river run. This is the difference between having a body that can meet your needs on the river and having one that cannot.

CHAPTER TWELVE

Perfecting Your Rodeo Body

There is no size or weight that is perfect for rodeo. The perfect rodeo body is one that is immune to most injuries, has power (strength and speed), and has ample muscle endurance for a full day of paddling.

PREVENTING INJURIES

Injuries come in two forms: overuse injuries and traumatic injuries.

Overuse Injuries
Sore wrist, especially after paddling

Cause: Often wrist pain is caused by the paddle grip you are using. If your paddle is slippery due to sunblock, a smooth shaft, or oily hands, you have to clamp down on the paddle too hard to prevent slippage. Wrist pain can also be caused by paddling a straight-shaft paddle. Straight shafts force you to pull harder on your pinky and smaller fingers because of the position of your hand and wrist when reaching forward for a forward stroke.

Solution: Electrical tape on the paddle shaft makes it easy to maintain a grip on the paddle. It is sticky but smooth enough not to cause blisters. Always use sand to wash any oil off your hands before paddling. Try a bent-shaft paddle.

Forearm and biceps soreness after paddling

Cause: Arm muscle soreness can be caused by a paddle shaft that is too stiff or a paddle that is too short. Short, jerky forward strokes can also lead to muscle soreness, as can a sudden increase in the amount or intensity of paddling.

Solution: Use a flexible shaft and blades. Keep your forward strokes even and long. Take anti-inflammatories to reduce swelling.

Shoulder tendinitis

Cause: This is usually a combination of traumatic and overuse injury caused by improper bracing, a stiff paddle shaft, lots of squirting, and tight neck muscles.

Solution: Keep your paddle in front of you, where you don't risk dislocation or high-stress positions of your shoulder. Keep inflammation down with anti-inflammatory medicine and ice to prevent further damage. Warm up and stretch your neck muscles every time you paddle.

Traumatic Injuries

Shoulder injury. It is impossible to guarantee that you won't hurt your shoulders when doing rodeo. There are too many variables to control 100 percent of the time. However, keeping your paddle in front of you and your power hand below your head is a start. You don't have to worry about hurting your shoulder unless you get your power hand over your head and behind you. Your nonpower hand is overhead all the time for proper strokes. Many people try to keep both hands down low. This is not necessary, but be aware of your hand and shoulder position.

The second most important way to prevent shoulder injury is to strengthen your muscles by doing rotator cuff exercises. These high-repetition exercises work the small rotator cuff muscles for shoulder stability. Although these muscles are small, they are used in all your paddle strokes. The large muscles around the shoulder (latissimus dorsi, pectoralis major, serratus anterior, and teres major) must also be strong to fully stabilize the shoulder joint. The strongest rotator cuff muscle in the world won't stop your shoulder from subluxing, dislocating, or getting hurt when you are holding onto a paddle and dealing with the power of the water. It is important to pack as much muscle mass around the shoulder as possible.

ROTATOR CUFF EXERCISES

1. With 6 to 8 pound dumbbells, pretend that you are drawing a sword from your belt and raising the sword high over your head to strike. Do this motion fifteen times, three sets, with both arms.
2. Using the same dumbbells, raise your arms from your side, thumbs up, to shoulder height. Hold them there for a count of three, go down slowly.
3. Same as number 2, but raise the dumbbells up in front of you.
4. Attach one end of a long, heavy rubber band to a doorknob or other fixed object. Hold your elbow against your side, gripping one end of the rubber band in one hand. Rotate your arm away from your body to the end of your range of motion. Work up to thirty repetitions for each shoulder. This exercise strengthens the external rotators of your rotator cuff.
5. Same as number 4, but start with your arm pointed out from your side (elbow against your side) and internally rotate your arm toward your abdomen. Work up to thirty repetitions on each side. This exercise strengthens your subscapularis, an internal rotator of the arm.

OTHER EXERCISES

1. *Dips:* Support your weight between two bars, two chairs, or the corner of a counter. Drop down and push yourself back up. Doing dips is critical to developing strength for rodeo and keeping the shoulders intact. Most strokes you take when kayaking are forward strokes. Dips work the opposite muscles, which happen to be cartwheel muscles. Dips pack muscle in front of your shoulder.
2. *Chin-ups:* Do as many as you can, for six sets. Chin-ups strengthen your latissimus and abdominal muscles and make for tighter shoulders. "Tight" here means no instability in the ball and socket joint, which causes strain on the tendons.
3. *Push-ups:* Do five sets of your maximum. This exercise must be done while keeping your shoulder muscles tight. Don't bounce or relax when going down. Improper push-ups cause your shoulder to open up and strain your tendons. Good push-ups strengthen your pectoralis major.

If you don't paddle every day, you need to do these exercises three times a week.

Rib injury. Cartwheeling has caused most of the top rodeo boaters to tear rib muscles. Your body isn't ready for cartwheeling until you strengthen the rib muscles. This can be done by cartwheeling, or you can do it in the gym. Most people don't paddle enough to ensure strong ribs without some out-of-boat exercises. All the top rodeo boaters have ribs of steel.

Lie on your back holding onto something stable with both hands. Swing your legs back and forth parallel to the floor. Don't let them touch the ground, and keep them straight. You should be able to do seventy-five or more for three sets. This will prepare your ribs for abuse on the water. If you get your ribs strong enough, you shouldn't be in danger of injury.

Neck injury. Weak, tight necks can cause lots of problems. Lie on your side and do head raises. Do fifty on each side. Then do fifty lying on your front and back. After that, stretch your neck sideways by twisting your head to the side and pulling your head to your chest. You should do this daily.

INCREASING POWER

Power is having strong muscles that can pull quickly. Pure strength isn't as useful as power. To increase power is as simple as paddling at full power often when you are out playing. The best time to improve your power is after washing out of a hole or off a wave. Most people hesitate, then slowly paddle back into the eddy. This is a bad habit and wasted training time. In a river-running situation, if you flip, you want to be able to roll up and catch the nearest eddy with no hesitation. This takes practice. The best time to practice this is when you are playing. Every time you wash out of a hole or wave, whether right side up or upside down, catch the eddy as high as you possibly can. This

means that you should roll quickly, then sprint to the eddy. Sprinting is a full-power, no-holds-barred charge into the eddy. There is no excuse not to. First, it is the best way to learn to roll quickly and get back in control immediately. Second, you develop a sense about where you are when you are underwater, so you don't make the mistake of rolling and paddling the wrong way. Third, you improve your muscle power quickly. You don't always want to be surfing holes or waves at full power. The sprint into the eddy is the best time for working on power. It saves you a trip to the gym. Practicing lots of flatwater or eddyline moves is good for power as well.

INCREASING MUSCLE ENDURANCE

Muscle endurance is improved through a combination of volume and intensity of paddling. The volume is simply how many strokes you take in a day. The intensity is how hard you are paddling. You should get off a river dead tired if you are trying to improve your muscle endurance. You usually are tired from lack of food, the long day, sitting in your boat, and so forth anyway. But this isn't the kind of tiredness that improves your muscle endurance. You should try to burn up all your physical energy by playing. If you have some energy left near the end of the river, stop at the last playspot and burn it up. Paddle until you feel like you won't be able to roll up if you don't stop. You can't measure how much energy you have when you get out of a hole after a ride; you always feel tired and out of breath then. When you are dead tired before you go into the hole, you may have had enough. It is possible to paddle on the river all day and not improve your muscle endurance or power at all if conserving energy on the river is your goal.

CHAPTER THIRTEEN

Exercising

In this chapter I offer a few exercises that can be done in the gym or at home for those of you who can't get on the water often enough to keep fit there. The key to being fit for kayaking is to have a well-rounded upper body, lower back, and neck. Flexible legs, lower back, neck, and torso keep you injury free and comfortable for long periods of time in the boat as well. Being fit means that you can play harder and longer than everyone else.

Warming up and Stretching. Being warmed up and at full range of motion before exercising (or paddling) hard is important for preventing injury. Doing some easy stretching after a five- to ten-minute warm-up is helpful. Stretching your torso, neck, and hamstrings is also important. These parts of your body usually get injured from lack of flexibility and overtiredness.

Rope climbing. Get a good thick rope, tie knots in it, and hang it from a tree. Climb it every day. Increase the speed and the number of times you can go up and down every few days. You will improve your ability to pull the boat forward, grip strength, and muscle endurance. Spend fifteen minutes on it a day.

Dips, chin-ups, and push-ups. See chapter 12.

Bent over rows. Using a heavy dumbbell (I use 75 pounds) put one hand and one knee on a bench and lift the dumbbell straight up as high as you can in sets of twenty. Three sets of twenty is ideal. If you can finish the third set, add weight. This is similar to taking forward strokes.

Flys. Lying on a bench, use dumbbells for flys. Be careful not to hurt your shoulders. Keep your shoulders tight when lowering the weights; don't let them relax and strain the rotator cuff muscles or tendons.

Grip strength. It is very disconcerting to feel your forearms get tired when playing in a hole. You don't want to have problems holding onto your paddle. There are lots of grip-strengthening exercises you can do at home. Find one you like.

Torso strength. There is a Nautalis machine designed specifically for strengthening your torso. If you go to a gym that has one, use it religiously to build bulletproof rib muscles. If not, do the leg-swinging exercise for rib injury prevention (see chapter 12).

I haven't lifted weights since 1995. This is because I paddle daily and tailor my training to achieve the results I need for an injury-free and effective paddling body. It is possible to acquire as much muscle mass as you could want simply by paddling.